23 Days

Also by Francis Bridger

A CHARMED LIFE

23 Days

A Story of Love, Death and God

FRANCIS BRIDGER

DARTON · LONGMAN + TODD

First published in 2004 by
Darton, Longman and Todd Ltd
1 Spencer Court
140–142 Wandsworth High Street
London SW18 4JJ

ISBN 0 232 52576 5

A catalogue record for this book is available from the British Library.

Designed and produced by Sandie Boccacci
using QuarkXPress on a G5 Apple PowerMac
Set in 10.5/13pt Bembo
Printed and bound in Great Britain by
Page Bros, Norwich, Norfolk

In loving memory

Renee W. Bridger

1945–2003

Contents

Acknowledgements

Not even a book as personal as this is a solitary effort; and so my thanks are due to all those who, in addition to my family, have shown their particular love and care over the last fourteen months. In doing so, they have enabled me to complete the task I resolved to undertake in those dark days of March 2003: Mike and Jill Adams, the Altadena Mission Team, LaRaine Alves, Ken Armitage, David Augsburger, Edward and Joanna Bailey, Bob and Sue Evens, John and Sonnie Goad, John Goldingay, Colin Harris, Reg and Judy Jones, Chuck and Shelby Larsen, Andrew Lucas, Terry and Shirley Miller, John Nolland, Kirsten Oh, Howard Peskett, Keith Peters, Catherine Ross, the people of St Mark's Altadena and St Michael's Winterbourne, Colville and Sylvia Smythe (and Jean), Michael and Valerie Taylor, the members of Trinity College Bristol, Karen West, Chris Weyermann, Rowan and Jane Williams, the Sijanczuk family. To them all I offer my deepest gratitude.

I also am grateful to Darton, Longman and Todd for affording me the opportunity to publish and for their editorial support throughout. To Virginia Hearn, Kathy Dyke and Helen Porter, I owe especial thanks for their sensitivity and patience.

FRANCIS BRIDGER

Prologue

I first met Renee Bosworth in the autumn of 1974. She was twenty-nine; I was twenty-three. Renee was the person I encountered as I walked through the door of Trinity College Bristol to begin my training for ordained ministry. As a resident student, her role was to allocate new students to their rooms. After I had talked with her, I knew I wanted to get to know this intelligent, forceful, pretty woman whose twinkling blue eyes, long brown hair, button nose and ability to hold her own in conversation captivated me from the start. Thus began an adventure that was to last almost twenty-nine years.

Six weeks after we met, I proposed and she accepted. Ten weeks later, we were publicly engaged. Seven months after that, we married: it was a rapid romance. In the quarter of a century that followed, Renee served as a lay parish minister, was subsequently ordained deacon, then priest, became the adoptive mother of three children and grandmother of two grand-children, travelled to Asia, Australia and the United States while disabled and finally returned to Trinity College as the Principal's wife. It was a life fully lived for God.

So when she died just twenty-three days after being diag-nosed with cancer, my world imploded. Renee had suffered from breast cancer four years before but had been clear of it for the last three. During this time, we had spoken frequently about the possibility of its coming back and had even expected it. But we had assumed that it would be the same type of cancer as before: slow-growing, straightforward to diagnose and treatable. It was on this basis that we had planned how to deal with it should it again make an appearance. Ironically, the one eventu-ality we didn't anticipate was the one that actually occurred: a rapid and aggressive cancer that was determined to take no prisoners and that the medical profession would prove unable to treat.

This book is the story of those twenty-three days and the months that followed. In part one, I tell of the period between Renee's diagnosis and death. Inevitably, it is a story of great sadness, but it is also one of faithfulness – the faithfulness of friends, colleagues, family and God.

In part two, I set out my thoughts as they appeared in the journal I kept while in the United States during April and May shortly after Renee's funeral. This was a time of unprecedented agony. I had nothing to do except grieve from the moment I woke in the morning to the moment I went to bed. To be sure, there were distractions; but essentially in these weeks I did more 'grief work' than I would have expected in a year had I been living my normal routine. But, by the grace of God, I was on a pre-planned sabbatical that lasted until the end of August – five months that had originally been scheduled for research but which, in the event, turned out to provide the space that enabled me to face the trauma of bereavement. At the time, it did not *feel* like a gracious gift, but even in the midst of intense pain, I knew it was. Paradoxically, it was when the pain felt at its most soul-destroying that the process of healing began.

My thoughts from this period do not make easy reading: I have been honest in expressing the reality of the feelings I recorded. But from the moment Renee died, I knew I had to keep a journal so that I could write about what had happened and offer reflections upon it. When I came to write up my notes in June and July, I did so with many tears. However, they were tears of healing as well as grief.

Part three records my later reflections on the issues that were raised during this time. They take the form of letters addressed to Alex, a figure who represents a composite of two people who have courageously and unfailingly walked with me on my journey and who have borne my sorrows when they have all but crushed me. To them I owe so much, not least my sanity, and to them I record my deepest gratitude. I would not be writing this today had it not been for their unbounded generosity and kindness. C and K (real initials) – you know who you are. You will always have my thanks.

It should be said that these letters raise difficult questions in ways that some readers may find disturbing. If that is the case, I hope they will accept my apologies but, at the same time, will respect my attempt to speak honestly. I have not sought to gloss over the intensity of the emotions of the past fourteen months; but neither have I written out of a desire to appear sensationalist. I have expressed what I have felt in the belief that it is far better to be honest about these things than to pretend to a false piety. If this helps others to be real about their grief as well, the book will have done its work. Nonetheless, the reader will be relieved to know that the intensity of those negative emotions has now passed and has given way to a stable reflectiveness that is the outcome of a movement from extreme grief (and all that entails) to a genuine hopefulness about the future. This is not to deny that periods of darkness will return – all the evidence from grief studies is that they will. But, to use a meteorological metaphor, the worst of the storm has passed. Heavy clouds may return from time to time and dump their load. But these will be short-lived by comparison; and when they appear, I know they will move on.

In the final chapter, I offer some brief reflections to leave the reader with seeds for continuing thought. When Renee went to meet her Lord, I determined that the cancer should not have the last word and that even in death her ministry should continue. This book is testimony to the redeeming work of God in enabling me to fulfil this desire and to honour the woman who was my wife for almost twenty-eight years. It is to her that I dedicate it.

FRANCIS BRIDGER
Ascension Day
20 May 2004

PART ONE

23 Days
Recalled

Days 1 to 5
Friday 7 February – Tuesday 11 February

'I'm sorry to tell you, Mrs Bridger, we have discovered cancer cells in your right lung and liver. We shall, of course, run further tests to determine the type and extent of the cancer but I'm afraid the cells are definitely present.' With these words, spoken just after noon on Friday 7 February 2003, the clock began ticking on the last weeks of Renee's life. Twenty-three days later she was dead.

Unless you have lived through it first-hand, to watch someone go from diagnosis to death in little more than three weeks is almost impossible to imagine. Even now, the recollection brings painful memories – and tears – flooding back. When the doctor delivered his diagnosis, nobody – not even he – had any idea how virulent the cancer would prove. Initially, the prognosis was hopeful. As Renee and I sat stunned by the news, the specialist spoke realistically and calmly of new 'smart' therapies that destroy only the cancerous cells in a person's system, not the healthy ones, thus leaving the patient in a much better state than older-style chemotherapy treatments. These new therapies, he assured us, were readily available and would be administered as soon as the exact type of cancer that had invaded Renee's organs could be identified. 'Once we know what we are dealing with,' he said, 'we'll be in a position to treat it.'

So confident was this prognosis that when I queried whether we should cancel our proposed sabbatical trip to the United States – only a few weeks away – he replied that it ought to be possible to fit in some outpatient chemotherapy sessions before we left and resume them, if necessary, after our return. To cancel would be premature.

Consequently, the decision Renee and I immediately faced was whom we should tell. As we talked, it became clear that we should let the news be known as widely as possible. We had seen in other, similar, cases the negative effects of undue secrecy; and although, on one hand, we wished our privacy to be respected, on the other we wanted our friends, family and colleagues to be brought into the picture. To anybody in a comparable situation, I would always advise the same: it may not be easy to share your *feelings* but at least share the *information*. The act of letting others know begins the process of coming to terms with the reality for yourself and so finding strategies to cope.

Looking back, I remain, even to this day, extremely glad we did so. It meant that we were enfolded in a network of love and prayer that stretched worldwide from the United Kingdom through Africa, Australia, the United States and Europe. To know we were cared for in this way was a tremendous reassurance.

But, from my point of view, there were additional reasons for telling people as much as possible. In the first place, it meant that future conversations could be conducted on the basis of openness and honesty. When anybody asked how Renee was, I was able to reply with the truth rather than evasion. This was a huge relief as the strain of trying to maintain a façade would have been intolerable. Secondly, it meant that people were praying from the vantage point of knowledge rather than speculation. This is surely healthier than leaving them to wonder what is going on. Thirdly, for those who are familiar with Myers-Briggs typology, I am an extravert who processes information by talking it through and who is energised by being with others rather than by retreating into myself. It was therefore very important for me to articulate my situation with people, to express my hopes and fears rather than bottle them up by internalising them. What an extravert most needs in the kind of situation I faced is not to be left alone but to be given the option to talk freely. If extraverts need time to themselves they will always ask for it. Finally – perhaps most obviously – sharing our situation led to an amazing amount of personal support which proved a

Godsend over the next three weeks and beyond. The out-pouring of love towards us both was deeply moving, overwhelmingly so at times.

So began the worst month of my life. To watch your wife decline and die, while all you can do is to look helplessly on, is a heartbreaking experience. A precious bloom shrivels before your eyes *and you can do nothing about it*. For such a thing to happen in the space of twenty-three days is devastating.

This is the story of a mysterious convergence of human and divine action in the midst of the most difficult crisis I have ever faced; it is also the story of those individuals who knowingly or unknowingly acted as channels of grace and healing both at the time and thereafter. To them all I remain inexpressibly grateful.

The Build-up

Although Renee had been admitted to hospital two days before receiving the diagnosis of cancer, she had been unwell for a number of weeks. Indeed, back in the previous November she had complained of a pain that felt like a cracked rib, but had refused to see her GP (primary care doctor) until January, when he sent her for an X-ray and subsequently diagnosed a chest infection. However, the antibiotics he prescribed failed to do the trick and by Wednesday 5 February, her breathing had become so laboured that she was taken into hospital for examination and tests. It was as a result of these that we learned the dreadful news of Friday the 7th.

Following the diagnosis, fluid was drained from Renee's lung and sent for analysis. Being the weekend, the hospital laboratory was closed, so we were given to expect the result on Tuesday. Tuesday came and went and still no result emerged. So the doctors suggested we return home and await their phone call. Once the outcome of the tests was known we would be notified of the process for arranging outpatient treatment. It all seemed straightforward and matter-of-fact. But, as I was to discover, there is no such thing where cancer is concerned. The situation is in constant flux. Nothing is ever completely predictable and everything is dependent on factors over which no one has control.

Some of these are systemic, such as the rate at which a laboratory is able to process test samples. Others are a matter of chance, such as whether a tissue sample will yield adequate results. Yet others have to do with human error. But perhaps the biggest unknown is the course that a disease will take. Throughout Renee's time in hospital, this was the most frustrating variable of all, and the one which ultimately led to the inability to formulate a treatment plan.

Put another way, the cancer simply never stood still. No sooner had the doctors begun to think they had got hold of it than it veered off in an unexpected direction. From the beginning, it moved so fast and spread so rapidly that it outpaced all attempts to catch it. To the end, it eluded analysis. Only as a result of the post-mortem examination were the pathologists able to identify exactly what killed Renee. At no stage during her illness were they able to do so. The frustration of not being able to treat the cancer was enormous.

Days 6 to 14
Wednesday 12 February – Thursday 20 February

Eight days after being taken into hospital, Renee returned home for the first and last time. On a chilly, grey February afternoon, escorted by myself and our daughter Rebecca (who had been able to combine a business trip from Nottingham with visiting us), she painfully and slowly re-entered our home. The infection had cleared up but Renee remained very weak. She could scarcely climb the stairs; and having done so, she remained in the bedroom for most of the time. Only once can I remember her coming downstairs: she was determined to see the early spring daffodils she had earlier planted in pots on the patio. She was too depleted to walk outside more than briefly but viewed them instead from inside. Even this small act gave her much pleasure.

The greatest sadness was to watch Renee gradually become a shadow of her former self. It was not that she physically wasted away; there wasn't time for that. Rather, she just got weaker and weaker as the combination of a chest infection and the rapidly spreading cancer so drained her that she could hardly move outside the bedroom. Indeed, as the illness progressed and she became increasingly unable to take more than a pace or two, the installation of a commode and the daily visits of a nurse became vital.

On Thursday, Rebecca left to return to her job. At this point, Renee was weak but stable. We joked and laughed. For a time, if I screened out the knowledge that she was stricken with cancer and ignored its visible effects, I could imagine that she was relatively normal and would recover.

However, we both knew the odds were starting to stack against us. Although we continued to talk about the sabbatical, it was noticeable that Renee now referred to it as a possible future event that might take place 'some day'. Gone were the high hopes of spring in California. In fact, we would both have been glad to see a few more weeks in Bristol, let alone Pasadena. After Renee died, a close friend emailed me to say that it was during this period that they had held a conversation in which Renee recognised she was dying but was hoping for a little longer.

When under stress, we often do extreme things. I attempted to drive a bargain with God. One evening after Renee had gone to sleep, I sat in the armchair and held a conversation with him along the following lines: 'Okay, Lord, here's the deal: what if you grant her six months – just long enough to pay one last visit to California – in return for my undivided attention for the rest of my life? It's surely not too much to ask, is it? Six months for umpteen years. Not a bad bargain.'

Fortunately, God was not prepared to do business. An extension of this kind would have broken our hearts as we went around doing things 'one last time'. I can now imagine what it would have been like visiting Renee's favourite beach in Malibu (a place called Paradise Cove), knowing that this would be the final visit. Or saying goodbye to dear friends, in the knowledge that we would never both visit them again. Looking back, I thank God that he was a lot wiser than I.

On Friday the 14th the cavalry arrived in the shape of Reg, an old friend from Nottingham. He and his wife Judy had been among our closest friends there and had visited us several times in Bristol. Indeed, when we moved to Trinity in November 1999, they took time off work to help us complete the move and settle in.

It so happened that Reg had been booked to come and stay for a week from the 21st to the 28th to keep Renee company while I was away at the Church of England's General Synod in London and afterwards at the enthronement of the new Archbishop of Canterbury. When we originally made this arrangement, long before we became aware that she had cancer, it was to reassure both Renee and myself that she would be okay during what would have been the longest period I had ever been away from home during Renee's years of disability. We both felt easier at the thought of somebody else being in the house. In the event, I didn't attend either Synod or the enthronement but Reg was a gift from God nonetheless: hearing the news of Renee's condition, he willingly brought his visit forward by a week to arrive on the 14th. While Renee continued to decline, he unstintingly helped me with the running of the household, sitting with her to give me a break, shopping, doing errands and all kinds of chores. In addition, his unfailingly gracious and cheerful manner kept our spirits up while his gentle realism enabled me to voice my deepest fears and expectations without falling into depression. I cannot thank him enough, even now. He was a sign and symbol of God's graciousness and mercy.

But, as Reg and I came to grips with the reality of caring for her, Renee slipped into greater and greater decline. She slept more, became increasingly immobile and showed less and less coherence. The doctor and district nurse started to visit each day. Pain medication was increased. With hindsight, the signs were writ large for all to see.

At the time, however, even the medics were unclear as to whether Renee's symptoms were side effects of the medication or evidence of the cancer's spread. What's more, there were still no firm results from the hospital tests. The samples kept on yielding inconclusive data. That Renee was suffering from cancer was not in doubt. But what kind of cancer, its speed and its likely course were still a matter of guesswork. All we could engage in was damage control.

Apart from the lack of treatment to stop the spread of the cancer, the most distressing feature to me was Renee's inability to take food or water. For some days, she had suffered from a thrush infection in the mouth which had resisted all medication. It simply got worse and worse to the point where she could take no nourishment at all. So desperate were Reg and I that we bought cans of all sorts – tapioca, semolina, fruit salad, anything – in the hope that she would at least take something. But the answer was always the same: 'Not now, maybe later.' In consequence, Renee became undernourished and severely dehydrated with swollen lips and a mouth filled with infection. It must have been agony.

Yet what was to be done to arrest her decline? As with so many medical situations, the symptoms were ambiguous. On the one hand, Renee's sleepiness and immobility might have been medication-related. On the other, they might have been the effects of the cancer's spread. Until the evidence became clearer, nothing could be done. And all the time, her life was ebbing away.

On Wednesday the 19th – one week after she had returned from hospital – Renee declined rapidly. She slept all day, could manage only brief, mumbled conversations, and refused all attempts at feeding. Most of the time, Reg or I simply sat by her bedside reading or praying silently. Although we didn't know it, this was to be her last full day at home. Even simple tasks such as helping her to the commode were a painful nightmare. In my heart of hearts, I knew this couldn't continue for much longer.

But in the evening, a delightful thing happened. Following the weekly service of Holy Communion at Trinity College, two women students – Jackie Taylor and Hilary Rundle – brought consecrated bread and wine to the house and shared in a short service around Renee's bedside. I have described this in detail later, so will not repeat it here; but suffice to say that this was another of God's mercies. That Renee and I were able to share in Communion together one last time was an experience that will remain with me and for which I will always remain thankful. Since the Eucharist is, theologically, a foretaste of the heavenly banquet that awaits us all in eternity, the symbolism, on reflection, was extremely powerful and moving.

The next day Renee started to turn yellow as the cancer attacked her liver with a vengeance. Although conscious for some of the time, she was increasingly weak and unable to speak. Severe dehydration had begun to take its toll. Consequently, when the doctor (a different doctor from the one who had been visiting to date) arrived in the afternoon, she immediately sent for an ambulance to take Renee back into hospital. Confused, Renee seemed unsure as to what was happening. But, quietly out of earshot in the garden, I asked the doctor the question I had been dreading all along: was Renee's condition now terminal?

At first, the doctor seemed surprised I had asked outright (presumably, this isn't what people usually do) but she answered honestly: 'I think you should prepare yourself that this might be the case.' She was, of course, rightly cautious in her assessment, since she could only offer a conclusion drawn from visual observation rather than laboratory tests. But I was grateful for her candour. Now, at least, I could orientate myself around the possibility that Renee was facing her last days. We would both need courage and grace.

A short time later, the ambulance arrived and Renee left our home for the final time. Subsequently, I learned she had voiced to a friend who had visited the house that she knew she would never return.

The next few hours were a whirlwind. By this time, Reg's wife Judy had arrived and we all spent the remainder of the evening at the hospital trying to determine what would happen next. At about 8.00 pm, I took the registrar who had admitted Renee to one side and asked for his professional opinion and prognosis. Initially, he was hesitant as the senior consultant had not yet examined her. However, eventually he answered: 'My best guess is that your wife has between one and seven days to live. I'm sorry to have to tell you this but that is the honest answer to your question.'

My reaction must have been obvious because he immediately emphasised that the consultant had not yet had the opportunity to make his own assessment. My first thought was: 'One day! Is that all we have? How can I get the children here in time?' The registrar must have read my mind for he suggested I contact them immediately.

Then came the second shock: he asked if I would think overnight about signing a do-not-resuscitate order. I knew what such things were but had not anticipated the question. The doctor carefully explained that they would want to know what to do in the event of Renee's organs failing. Should they try heroic measures to revive her, for example, if her heart were to arrest? Did I want them to attempt to bring her back?

My mind was reeling. Not only had I just learned that Renee might have only a day or two to live but I was also now being asked to pronounce on what to do when all else failed. Fortunately, I had no doubts: Renee had frequently said that she was not afraid of death and that she valued the quality of life far more than the quantity. She had no wish to linger on in some kind of impaired state, especially if she were in the last stages of terminality. Nonetheless, I needed time to organise my thoughts and emotions as I struggled to process this welter of information.

Then a thought struck me: how was I to make Renee aware of her condition? I was now in possession of information about the ending of her life that she didn't, at this stage, have. So I faced the prospect of having to tell her that she might have only a short time to live.

Trying to deal with these thoughts, I spent the rest of the evening helping Renee settle into the hospital ward. By now, she was aware of her surroundings and slightly more coherent. But she remained very weak and dehydrated. The immediate task was to get fluids into her and make her comfortable. I left late and promised to return the next morning in time for the visit of the consultant which was scheduled to take place any time after 11.00 am.

Days 15 to 18
Friday 21 February – Monday 24 February

On Friday, I awoke fearing the worst. I had phoned the children overnight and promised that I would contact them as soon as I had reasonably accurate news. They could be in Bristol within a few hours but it seemed best to wait until I had some hard information and had heard the consultant's prognosis.

To my astonishment, when I arrived at her bedside on Friday morning, Renee was sitting up, had eaten and was talking normally. The junior doctor explained that many of the outward symptoms I had observed the previous day were the result of dehydration and that now Renee was receiving fluids intravenously, she was much more alert. I was relieved that at least we could talk and that she would be able to take part in the conversation with the consultant.

At about midday, he arrived and chatted in a clear but relaxed manner about the situation. He reiterated that it was still proving impossible to identify the cancer with precision and so he proposed a liver biopsy, to take place on Monday or Tuesday. This would provide a tissue sample that could be tested with accuracy. In the meantime, the medical staff would build up her strength and administer a powerful drug to deal with the thrush.

As to the prognosis, the consultant was careful, I noted, to outline a range of possible courses of action. In this, he was thoroughly professional and honest. He didn't hide from Renee the seriousness of her condition; but on the other hand, he did not rule out treatment such as chemotherapy (once the biopsy results had identified the type of cancer). Significantly, he now also made mention of palliative care – a sign that he was beginning to sow the seed in our minds that a later diagnosis might indicate treatment to be impossible.

Once he had left, Renee and I talked at length. As far as I could tell, she understood what the consultant had said. However, I remained unsure about how far she had grasped that her illness might now be terminal. So I kept quiet until I had had the chance to talk either with the consultant or his registrar.

When a little later in the day I was able to speak with the doctor who had admitted Renee the previous evening, I asked what had happened to the one to seven day prognosis and the DNR order. His reply was instructive: 'Your wife has improved significantly as a result of rehydration, so Mr Harvey (the consultant) would rather wait until after the biopsy before coming to a view on either issue.'

I was by now both relieved and confused. What interpretation should I put on the situation? How optimistic – or pessimistic – should I be? These were the questions running around my head. Nevertheless, with Reg and Judy's help, I decided we should contact Simon, Rebecca and Samantha to suggest they come the next day. At the same time, we alerted those closest to us in Bristol, Nottingham and elsewhere that it would be advisable to visit as soon as possible.

Over Renee's last conscious weekend, friends arrived by the carload. By the end of Sunday, almost everybody we could reasonably expect had appeared – so much so that I wondered at what point Renee would realise what was happening. But if she did so, she never showed it. Even when our three children arrived on Saturday armed with flowers and chocolates, she simply burst into tears and welcomed them with literally open arms. They, in turn, showered her with love and laughter. It was a wonderfully moving experience. I was very proud of them.

But, at the same time, I became increasingly worried by another development. From time to time throughout the weekend, Renee drew me to one side quietly and told me of her growing concern that 'something terribly wrong' was taking place on the hospital ward. When I asked what she meant, she replied with statements such as: 'Don't ask too many details. It's too dangerous.'

As Saturday and Sunday wore on, these kinds of conversation between us became more frequent and urgent in tone. At one point on Sunday, Renee talked about 'forces of evil' let loose at night and even alluded to the mysterious death of a patient. However, when I checked, there had been no deaths on the ward at all. During one particular conversation, she looked hard at the other side of the ward and asked me if I could see demonic beings dancing in a circle. When I replied that I couldn't, she commented that I hadn't been given the insight to see them.

By now, it had become obvious to me that either Renee's medication was causing these delusions or that the cancer had spread to her brain. On Sunday evening, I made a mental note to raise the matter with the consultant the next day.

But I was never to do so. On Monday morning, the hospital called to say that Renee was in a great deal of pain but was refusing to take her medication since she believed the staff were trying to poison her. For the first time, the word paranoia was used.

Judy and I rushed in (Reg had meanwhile returned briefly to Nottingham) to find Renee screaming in agony, clutching her midriff. Only as I gently reassured her that she was safe, did she take her medication. So great was the pain by now, however, that the staff had to administer a massive dose of liquid morphine to get it under control. Unfortunately, this put Renee into an unconscious state from which she failed to recover. She never spoke to me again. No treatment was now possible. The beginning of the end had arrived.

But it was not yet the end. A morphine syringe driver attached to her arm pumped controlled amounts of the drug into her bloodstream at pre-set intervals. This kept her comfortable and without pain but unconscious for the final week of her life.

From that moment on, I resolved that Renee should not die alone. However long she might have remaining, I was determined there should always be someone she loved at her side. When Reg returned later that day (Judy, meanwhile, had to go back to Nottingham for work and to care for her elderly mother), he readily agreed with my wish and together we worked out a plan. Consequently, there was never a time of day or night when Renee was not accompanied by someone she loved. This was to be the pattern until her death the following Sunday.

Days 19 to 23
Tuesday 25 February – Sunday 2 March

During the six days that ensued, a great deal happened – so much so that I can only give highlights here. On Tuesday, Simon and Sam came (Rebecca was ill). Together, they, Reg and I slept around Renee's bed all night on chairs provided by the hospital staff who were wonderfully kind in providing us with food and drinks. Renee remained unconscious; but we snatched at sleep in fits and starts. Throughout the night we were interrupted, sometimes hilariously, by unintended comments from other patients.

One of these involved an elderly woman conducting a conversation out of sight with what we supposed to be a member of the nursing staff. Only later did we realise there had been nobody present except the woman herself. The entire discussion – about a man she had loved some years before – had been carried on in her sleep with a purely imaginary respondent! Another lady embarked at regular intervals on counting sheep out loud. She would start at number one and work her way up to the early hundreds. The only problem was that she always stumbled at ninety-nine, so we could never be sure she would get past a hundred. When she couldn't manage it, she went back to number one all over again. When she scaled a century, the count continued until she either fell asleep or got to a hundred and twenty or thereabouts and then went back to the beginning. Yet another elderly woman put herself on the commode behind curtains in the early hours of the morning and promptly fell asleep. And so it went on. We found ourselves suppressing giggles at the surrealism of the situation.

Simon and Sam had to return to Nottingham on Wednesday morning but promised to return as soon as needed. By this time, it had become clear that Renee had stabilised and was likely to continue in a similar condition for the foreseeable future. So it was that I began to plan her funeral. Sitting at her bedside, I talked with Renee about the details of the service (although of course she couldn't respond). She had chosen the hymns some years before but hadn't confided in me where she had written them down. I could only recall two of them, so in the end added two more which I knew she liked. I still have to this day the notebook in which I wrote the outline of the service.

Looking back, I remain glad that, although Renee was

unconscious the whole time, I nonetheless decided to discuss her funeral with her as if she were a conscious participant in the conversation. The doctors regarded it as important to talk to her, since the hearing function is often the last to cease. Other visitors accepted this and included her in any conversation they held with me or among themselves. One particularly moving moment occurred when I came to the ward one morning to discover Esther, a young Zimbabwean ordinand at Trinity to whom Renee had been spiritual director, quietly singing hymns into Renee's ear. Later, Esther wrote to me the following:

> Once when I was singing *How Deep the Father's Love*, Renee squeezed my hand. I also began to read to her from Julian of Norwich ... about God's will and she opened her eyes and said to me, 'That's what I want, God's will.'

To know this, even now, brings great comfort.

Day by day, the week passed. On Thursday, Rowan Williams was enthroned as Archbishop of Canterbury. Strange though it might seem, I thought at the time this might be the moment Renee would choose to die. So I half-jokingly said to her on Thursday evening, 'Okay Renee, Rowan's enthroned now. You can go if you want. It's all done.' Although said in jest, I would not have been surprised if she had taken me at my word. But she had other ideas.

Renee had now been moved to a private room off the main ward. This was a sure sign that she was not expected to live much longer. Consequently, I phoned Simon and Sam (Rebecca was still sick) and suggested they might not have much longer if they wanted to see Renee again. They arrived on Thursday evening and left the next morning: another night spent in vigil.

On Friday, the consultant visited and declared that he was surprised Renee had managed to hang on so long, given the rate at which the cancer was eating at her organs. To be sure, her liver was now severely swollen and she looked yellow as it continued to fail. But, as he noted, Renee had been physically strong, despite her disability; and the speed of the cancer had been so great that she had not had time to waste away. Her body had reserves to draw on. Nonetheless, he would be surprised if she were still alive on Monday.

And so it proved. After a terrible Friday night, in which I spent the whole time vomiting, the hospital staff sent me home to get some sleep. As Judy was able to return to Bristol on Saturday morning, Reg took the opportunity to do the same. We came back to the vigil on Saturday evening.

However, the nurses were insistent that I get a good night's sleep, so they found me a relatives' room off a nearby ward in which I could stay overnight. They promised that they would send for me if any change were to occur.

In the event, this was to be another of God's gracious provisions. At 7.00 am on Sunday morning I was awoken with a vigorous knocking and a voice urging me to make my way as soon as possible to Renee's room. In my dressing gown, I ran as fast as I could, to find Reg and Judy at her bedside.

From the sound of Renee's breathing, it seemed obvious that we were near the end. When I said as much to the attending nurse, she confirmed it. The moment we had been fearing had finally arrived.

Just over an hour later, Renee passed into the presence of her Lord at 8.34 am on Sunday 2 March 2003, the Lord's day, the day of resurrection, the Feast of the Transfiguration. She and God had at last decided the wait should end. It was time for her to move on. But even in that last hour, the graciousness of God could be seen. The fact that I had been sleeping in the hospital meant that the three of us were able to say goodbye in the way we wanted. We sat around Renee's deathbed enabling her to make what in bygone times would have been called a 'good death'. We read the scriptures together (Revelation 21, Psalm 23 and John 14); we read extracts from Renee's beloved Julian of Norwich and liturgy from the Anglican service for the dying. Finally, I anointed her with oil, said the Lord's Prayer and commended her into God's hands. A few seconds later, she breathed her last and gave up her spirit. We sat silently weeping. The twenty-three days were over.

Postscript I

A few days after Renee's death, Michael Taylor, a friend and former clergy colleague from the parish in which I had served in Nottingham, sent me the following. He was unaware that Renee was at the point of death at the time of the incident:

> On Sunday 2 March, I was due to preach at the 8.30 am service at St Wilfrid's, Calverton. Just before the service began, I was able to have a short time of quiet. During this, I was thinking about my sermon and the significance of the Transfiguration. Then in my mind's eye, I had an image of the Transfiguration but the picture was not of Christ.
>
> The picture was of a radiant Renee in clothes of dazzling white. She was serene and clearly without pain. She was smiling. I felt completely at peace with this image as I had been praying that God would release Renee from her pain. Shortly after this our service began. The time of Renee's death was about 8.35 am – not long after I had my vision.
>
> It is unusual for me to have 'pictures' of this sort.

In the weeks that followed, Michael's vision proved to be another of those small mercies sent by God.

Postscript II
Tuesday 11 March

It was a cold, windy, wet winter afternoon as around 250 people gathered in a small country church on the outskirts of Bristol to give thanks for Renee's life and ministry and to commit her to the grave. This was the parish in which she had begun her ministry twenty-seven years before. Astonishingly, the rector was the same man who had trained her back then, Canon Dr Edward Bailey who, with his wife Joanna, has been a good friend in the months since Renee's death. Edward spoke with feeling and dignity about the 'remarkable circularity' of Renee's having ended her ministry in the church where she started.

Other friends spanning the whole of Renee's adult life came forward to give testimony to her ministry. A fellow student who trained with her at Trinity in the 1970s; a teacher from the inner-London parish in which we served from 1978 to 1982; friends from Nottingham days; the wife of a Trinity faculty member who became Renee's closest friend in Bristol after 1999; and, not least, the rector and his wife from St Mark's Altadena, the California parish Renee and I attended whenever we were in Pasadena. They flew over especially to be at the funeral and, a few weeks later were to take me into their home during the period I was in California.

The sermon was given by an old friend Jonathan Gledhill – then Bishop of Southampton, now Bishop of Lichfield – who had been the student president at Trinity while Renee had been student vice-president in the early 1970s. He spoke of her sense of fun, her robust faith and the trustworthiness of God. It was a fitting tribute and a powerful word from the Lord.

The Trinity choir sang 'Jesu, Joy of Man's Desiring' (one of Renee's favourites); Jackie Searle, Dean of Women, led the congregation in prayers; Howard Peskett, Vice Principal, read from Julian of Norwich; Rebecca and Sam read from C. S. Lewis and the New Testament respectively. I spoke a tribute on behalf of the four of us. Simon acted as a pallbearer.

Then it was all over. We filed out of the church to the graveside where Renee's coffin was lowered into its resting place. The short act of committal ended with a prayer of hope that God would give us all comfort 'in this world and the next'. Floral tributes were laid. And so, thirty-two days after she had been diagnosed with cancer, we bade farewell to the woman I had loved for almost twenty-nine years. As her gravestone was subsequently to say: 'Wife, mother, grandmother, priest. "Not here but risen."'

PART TWO

A Grief Told

For a year prior to her death, Renee and I had been planning a five-month sabbatical beginning in March 2003. She was excited about this and had spent months in anticipation of our having more time together at home and at Fuller Theological Seminary, Pasadena where I had held a summer teaching position since 1999 as visiting professor of pastoral care and counselling. The dry southern Californian climate was perfect for Renee's disability and each time we visited, her condition improved rapidly. We both held deeply fond memories of the place and the people, many of whom had become good friends over the years.

The decision I therefore faced after Renee had died was whether to start the sabbatical as planned or whether to abandon the project altogether. In the end, I decided to go to Fuller – but with deep misgivings. For one thing, I was so exhausted that I could hardly carry out the theological research I had originally scheduled. For another, how would I cope six thousand miles away from friends and family? But there was nothing to be gained by staying at home and our friends in Pasadena made it clear that they would welcome me and would offer their support as I embarked on my grief journey.

In the weeks that followed, I recorded my reactions to Renee's death in a journal – the first I have ever kept. The entries reflect the intensity of those weeks in which my raw emotions poured themselves onto page after page. It was a time of profound spiritual engagement and insight as I struggled with God, with my humanity, with my feelings of loss and abandonment and with the theological questions generated by the devastating experiences of the previous two months.

Friday 28 March
(five days before leaving for the USA)

Renee used to have a saying when people asked how painful her disability was: 'Good days, bad days.' The trouble with grief is there are no good days, only ones that are less bad. Most of the time it's just plain awful: a never-ending sorrow that eats away at your guts.

It's not a matter of regrets for what we didn't manage while she was alive. I can cope with that. No, it's the heartbreaking awareness of *what will never be*, the dreadful fact of having to reorder my life around one simple truth – that there will never again be any of the things that only a few weeks ago we took for granted: conversation at the end of the day, playing with the dogs, eating out, discussing theology, taking holidays, watching TV, going to the movies, sharing books, meeting friends, arguing about politics, making love. In short, all those things that married couples do. All that *we* expected to do for some years yet.

Now they've all died along with Renee. They're every bit as vanished as she is. And I hate it. Not a tiny hate but an all-consuming hate. The kind of hate that I imagine could drive you insane, because I still find it impossible to believe that I shan't do any of those things again with the woman I loved for almost twenty-nine years. But that's the horrible truth and it stares me in the face everywhere I look – so much so that some days it's tempting not even to get up. After all, I can't be confronted with the things other couples do if I don't step outside the house.

But the dog[1] still has to be walked. So I *will* get up.

Monday 31 March

Flying to the States tomorrow. I don't know whether to welcome or dread it. At the moment, I feel as if I want to do both. I know it's going to be painful but there really is no choice if I

---

[1] The observant reader will have noticed that I have just referred to two dogs. This is explained by the fact that four days after Renee's funeral, the dog she had chosen as a puppy fourteen years earlier died of heart failure.

am to honour Renee. I've always disliked it when people say after a death 'It's what he/she would have wanted.' How can they be sure? But in this case, I know that keeping to our plans is exactly what she would want. Besides, I owe it to our friends to see them as soon as possible.

So on Tuesday 1 April, I flew from London to Los Angeles. Ironically, we first got to know LA when we took a holiday at Fuller following treatment Renee received in 1998 for the first bout of cancer.

Friday 4 April

I've been reading the grief manuals. They're crap. Sometimes helpful crap – but crap nonetheless. Knowing the anatomy of grief and the nature of the grieving process does absolutely nothing to lessen the agony. You might as well suppose that knowing the physiology of your leg will somehow take the pain away when a bus runs over it.

Likewise, knowing that *on average* (note the implied caveat) people take between eighteen months and three years to grieve doesn't make it any easier to bear here and now. I don't want to be told that I shall one day be ready to 'reinvest' my energies in a new life and possibly a new relationship. It makes it sound as if my love for Renee is no more than a commodity to be played on the stock market. I want to have the opportunity to share my love with *her*, not somebody else once I have 'moved on'. It's all well and good for the experts to reassure me that what I'm feeling is normal and healthy (I knew that already); but how many of them have actually *known* the agony, the sheer sense of powerlessness, that comes from watching your wife die in only twenty-three days; or the terrible feeling when you have caught her final breath on your cheek and kissed her just-dead lips; or have gently closed her eyelids as if pulling down the shutters on a suddenly empty room? I quite see how people rush into all kinds of activities just to do something about the pain. I can even see why some take their own lives – not that I have any intention of doing so. After all, when there is no prospect that the person you have loved absolutely and deeply for so long will ever be your lover again, life seems pretty pointless. The experts might know this, in the same way that theologians know what other theologians have said about heaven. But how many have actually been there?

Saturday 5 April

How best to characterise grief? I wish I could say it does nothing more hurtful than follow you around like a stray dog that happens to cross your path and wanders off again while you're out for an afternoon stroll. But it's much more insidious and vicious than that. Grief has only one goal: to usurp your lover's place. It wants to become your new companion, your new best friend. This is what it lusts after.

But – and here's the real cruelty – it doesn't even *attempt* to play the seductress, enticing you into its presence with promises of consolation. No, it waits in hiding until it can steal up, knock you to the ground and stamp all over you as you writhe in agony. Then it delights in kicking the living hell out of you until your guts are bursting and you can take no more, leaving you a sobbing wreck crying out in desperation for your loved one to hold you in her arms and make everything right.

But, of course, she can't.

How I hate that bloody cancer.

Monday 7 April

I looked up at the San Gabriel mountains this morning and wept. They were bathed in a brilliant sunshine backed by a dazzling blue sky. It was a perfect morning. Except … except Renee wasn't there to enjoy it. And never will be again. This was supposed to be the start of our sabbatical – six weeks in

Pasadena enjoying the Californian spring and the climate that did her disability so much good. She absolutely adored the place. She was pain-free here. Now she's without pain but she's not here. I can't escape the irony. It seems too cruel for words.

I was looking through her spiritual journal for 2000 the other day and came across some Pasadena postcards. They were followed by a single handwritten phrase: 'Pasadena, home from home.'

Where is home? I'm not asking a metaphysical question in the way that people ask 'Where is heaven?' I'm just wondering what we mean by 'home'. The obvious answer for me is that my home is in Bristol. But that's only the house I live in, isn't it? As far as I'm concerned, home is where Renee is – and that's not Bristol or anywhere else, except that her remains lie in a grave a few miles outside the city. The Renee I knew, the woman I loved, is in eternity, outside time and space. She's resurrected. Her home is there, not here. So you see why I don't know how to answer the question? I'm *homesick* but I don't know what that means.

I'm not functioning in theological mode yet. So although I know all the stuff about being pilgrims and strangers in this world and our true home being heaven, these are just words. It's not that I don't believe them or that I think the ideas are old-fashioned or an insult to intelligence. If anything, the opposite is true: when you're grieving, it's the simplicity of imagery and metaphor that helps the most – even for someone like me who works mostly with complex prose. Those who dismiss biblical talk of heaven as childish are either completely unimaginative or have no idea of what it's like to be pulled apart by grief. The cold language of scientific realism is totally useless at times like these.

The experts talk about being ready to 'let go' your loved one and 'move on'. I'm sure they're right according to their lights but I can't help feeling we're back to the crap factor again. That I'll be able to adjust to a new life in due time, I don't doubt. As far as I can tell, I'm 'grieving healthily', if the forests of Kleenex I've got through are anything to go by. My tear ducts have never known themselves worked so hard.

But I refuse (yes, *refuse*) to speak as if somehow I can cast Renee off like an old barge ready to be let go from its moorings so that it can drift out to sea and sink. She was the (human) centre of my life for almost twenty-nine years, for goodness' sake! I can't just let her slip away into the mists. I'm not in denial that she's dead – it's hard to do that when you've watched somebody die – and I don't intend to erect any shrines to her. When I'm ready, I'll sort out her clothes and personal belongings, even though it will open the wounds all over again.

But I'm damned if I'll adopt the language of 'letting go' and 'moving on'. She'll always be a part of my life, not as a past memory but as a continuing presence as I seek to integrate her into my continuing life rather than behave as if she's no longer a reality.

Tuesday 8 April

It's exactly four weeks since I buried Renee in the corner of an English country churchyard in the lee of the church where she began her parish ministry in 1976. At the funeral service, the rector called this a divine circularity. I suppose it is. She's ended where she began.

But why are four weeks important (or five, or six, or however many)? There's something about time that seems to be hardwired into the human psyche. Kant would call it a fundamental structure of the mind. For some reason we seem to embed important occasions chronologically in our subconscious without realising what we've done. They then clamour for our attention at regular, pre-determined intervals like today.

So it is that I've been wandering around Pasadena remembering and weeping by turns. Remembering the old familiar places – the bookshops, the cafés, the shops, the seminary campus –

where we used to hang out; and weeping that it was only a month ago that marked an end to all the possibilities we'd hoped for. The contrast couldn't be greater. It rips me apart.

The experts call this the 'yearning and searching' stage. This, at least, is true. I can't stop visualising Renee from the moment I wake up to the moment I go to sleep. Not surprisingly, C. S. Lewis captured it exactly: 'I am thinking about her nearly always. Thinking of [her] words, looks, laughs and actions … Her absence is like the sky, spread over everything.'[2]

For me, it fills every horizon too.

What this does is leave me with a nagging sense of 'ought-ness'. Not the kind of 'ought' that stems from duty unfulfilled (back to Kant again) but an 'ought' that protests: 'She ought to be here, she ought to be doing *this*, she ought to be enjoying *that*. The universe ought not to be like this.' And as with all 'oughts' the emotional pressure is enormous and unceasing.

Logicians tell us with absolute certainty that we can't derive an 'ought' from an 'is'. But I can: Renee *is* not here. But she *ought* to be.

II

Went to the Fuller prayer garden as part of my wanderings this morning. It seemed strange not pushing Renee there in her wheelchair, for she loved its ambience – quiet, peaceful, prayer-ful. She used to sit facing the fountain for an hour or so, meditating, praying, interceding. I can quite see why she loved it.

But I couldn't meditate today. The place was too permeated with her absence. To meditate would have required energy and concentration; and I don't have much of either at the moment. All I could do was let my inner thoughts rise to the surface and follow wherever they might lead – a jumbled stream more charged with emotion than structured and coherent.

[2] C. S. Lewis, *A Grief Observed* (London: Faber & Faber, 1978), p. 13.

Sometimes they led to more thoughts; at other times to a mental pause; at yet others to tears. Lots of tears. Neither could I pray in the conventional sense. The words just wouldn't come. Not that I felt (or feel) alienated from God: I simply couldn't assemble myself mentally or spiritually. All I could do was to rest in God, surrounded by the beauty of the garden and let him have my confused and disconnected ponderings.

The comforting thing is that I felt at one with Renee, sitting where she sat, looking at features she enjoyed, trying to do what she used to. This garden touched her soul and for a few minutes it touched mine too.

Carved on the wall behind the fountain was a verse from Scripture: 'As the hart panteth after the water brooks, so panteth my soul after Thee, O God' (Psalm 42:1, KJV). But my soul doesn't pant after *God* – it pants after *her*.

Lord, as I sit here how should I pray? Surely not for her soul? Not for her 'blessed repose'? She's already enjoying resurrection life. She doesn't need my prayers.

But somehow I do want to pray for her, even though every theological instinct within me rejects the idea.

Lord, I don't know how to pray: help Thou my lack of prayerfulness.

Am I wanting to use prayer in this garden, this place where she met so deeply with you, as some kind of way of getting a message to her? Does my subconscious think of this as a doorway between heaven and earth, the equivalent of the wardrobe that leads to Narnia?

Lord, when you see her, please tell her how much I love her and miss her. I do so want her to know.

Wednesday 9 April

Tomorrow I'm going for the first of six sessions of grief counselling. The enormity of what's happened over the last two months has begun to bite and I know that if I'm to grieve healthily I need some professional help. After all, that's exactly what I tell others; so I can hardly run away from my own advice.

It will be with G, a Christian man of depth and compassion, whom I've known for some years and trust implicitly. Funnily enough, when I approached him, he said it had been his intention to make the offer but wasn't quite sure whether I'd welcome it. That makes me feel a bit better. But I'm still fearful of what state it will leave me in. Nonetheless, there's no turning back now.

Friday 11 April

I thought I was making progress in my grief until my meeting with G yesterday. He is a first-rate counsellor but I still came away shredded and spent the rest of the day in tears. Even now, twenty-four hours on, it still feels bleak. Maybe I've just been fooling myself.

I've known all along that I would have to undertake the grief journey. That's why I asked for G's help in the first place. I've seen enough blocked grief in my ministry to know that those who grieve best are those who seek help.

But, oh, the pain! Is the whole journey going to be like this? If so, I don't know if I can stay the course. As I read the literature, it seems it can only get worse. God help me.

We looked at two metaphors that seemed to fit my situation: (a) the abyss; (b) the journey to Gethsemane. Both are awful. The image of the abyss puts me at the edge of a chasm the width of the Grand Canyon, looking across to the other side. That's where the future lies but it's too wide to leap. So I stand at the edge, staring down into an apparently bottomless pit. It's so dark I can't see how deep it is. The only way to get over the chasm is to climb all the way down and then all the way up again. Not till then I will have come through the grief process and be ready to build a new life.

Most people, it seems, take one look at the abyss and run away. The prospect of the climb down and up again is just too painful. So they avoid it by all means possible: distraction, denial, inappropriate relationships – anything that will take them away from the edge. 'After all,' they reason, 'why should I put myself through even more agony?'

I know how they feel.

As if that weren't bad enough, there's Gethsemane as well. According to this, I must tread the path which Jesus trod, all the way through loneliness, despair, fear and abandonment. 'If it be possible, take this cup from me; but if not, then not my will but thine' (Matthew 26:42). This, I guess, is a theologisation of grief theory. And since I have only just begun the journey, the rest to come looks pretty dreadful. Only when I reach the acceptance stage – 'not my will but thine' – will I be able to look forward in hope. I'm nowhere near that yet. Will I ever be? My head says 'Yes' but my heart yells 'No!'

The trouble is: on the basis of either metaphor, running away doesn't work. The grief is never dealt with. It's either blocked or at some point in the future it rises up like a phoenix and starts eating away at whatever new life the mourner has managed to build. Unresolved grief is apparently very good at destroying new marriages.

So it seems I have no choice but to begin climbing down into the abyss; to go all the way to Gethsemane. No wonder I feel shredded and terrified. Is this all I have to look forward to for months – if not years – to come?

The worst thing is that I must do it alone. That's the message of the Gethsemane story. The disciples went with Christ but failed at the last. While he was agonising, they fell asleep. It wasn't that they didn't care – of course they did. But they couldn't feel what he felt and they didn't have the stamina. So although others may walk with me, I don't know if I can depend on them in the end. For only I can do my own grieving, only I can feel *my* pain. Only I can know the loss of *my* wife. Friends may grieve with me but they can't grieve in my place. They'll have their own grief to bear but it won't be mine.

This fills me with unspeakable dread. Not only have I got to go through it all, but I'm the only one that can do it for me. And even if somebody were willing to journey with me in these next few weeks, when the pain will be at its most excruciating and when I'm going to be spilling my guts all over the place, who will it be? It would need to be someone who cared enough to go through the agony alongside me, to feel it as I do, and who won't run away when the pain becomes unbearable. Who is there that would be willing to put themselves through *that*? It would be a remarkable act of love. My closest friends would do it but they're back home; and the one person who would have accompanied me without hesitation on such a journey is the very reason I've got to go to Gethsemane in the first place. What an irony.

II

I've thought about this and I haven't really got any choice. I'm going to have to take the risk of asking someone here to be my fellow-traveller. (Not, I hasten to add, to become my disciple!) But whom can I trust? Whoever it is has got to be willing to see me vulnerable and exposed and not be shocked. In turn, I've got to take the risk of entrusting myself to someone who hardly knows me. And they've got to be somebody with whom I won't feel humiliated when I collapse. It's like asking a stranger to see me naked. What's more, I'll have to trust them to be strong enough to cope. It's a huge thing to ask of any but my oldest and closest friends. And they're not available. But what else can I do? I can't just retreat into myself. That would be disastrous. But who *is* there?

Saturday 12 April

I've only had three dreams about Renee since she died. The first was terrifying: she was running – limping, actually – into the kitchen of our house from the back garden, crying for help, pursued by two men in black. I managed to wrestle the first to the floor but the second jumped over me and grabbed her. The last thing I heard was a soul-wrenching scream.

Then I woke up.

The symbolism couldn't be more obvious: the men in black were the cancer. I tried to stop them but I was powerless. No matter what I did, the cancer got her in the end.

I can't remember the second dream so it must have been pretty benign.

But last night I had the most important dream so far: we had recently moved into a large house with a spacious basement for books, CDs, magazines and so on. But the basement was disorganised. So one day, while at work, I decided on a plan to straighten it out. At the end of the day I rushed home – almost getting myself killed in the process – only to find that Renee had unilaterally taken it upon herself to reorganise the room while I was out.

Wow, was I annoyed because she had done this without discussing it with me first (never mind that I had proposed to do the same)! What's more, she had arranged things *exactly* as I would have. The books and magazines were perfect. This made it all the more galling.

In other words, *she had got there before me.*

The dream ended.

My feelings were so strong that they woke me up at 5.19 am (I looked at the clock). For a split second I found myself thinking: 'Now I'm gonna give her a piece of my mind!', and turned to speak to her.

Then I realised what I was doing: I was about to get angry with a dead woman.

When I reflect on the meaning of this dream, several points occur to me. First, the dynamics are utterly realistic. Renee did occasionally decide on a course of action and go for it without discussing it with me. And I reacted as in the dream: annoyance (so what else is new between married couples?). Secondly, and perhaps most importantly, the dream marks a turning point in the way I think of Renee: I'm no longer idealising her. She's off the pedestal on which I put her at death. She's the real Renee once more, irritating traits and all. And I'm the real husband: not permanently adoring but sometimes peeved and with equally irritating traits. Thirdly, the fact that I woke up ready to tell her how much she had got under my skin shows that I'm relating to her once more as in real life, with all the flaws and foibles we both possessed. There's a reality about the dream that makes me see I have somehow moved on, though how far remains to be seen.

Sunday 13 April

I've been racking my brains as to who might be my companion on the grief journey and have decided to ask P to consider it. I feel nervous about doing so as it's a lot to ask of anyone, let alone someone who doesn't know me that well. But there's nobody else with the same kind of gifts whom I would trust. I'll ask but won't be surprised if the answer's no.

Monday 14 April

I miss Renee like crazy. It still seems all so unreal. Ten weeks ago we were looking forward to being here just as children look forward to Christmas. Now it feels bittersweet. Christmas has arrived but without the person who really counts.

The worst of it is that the misery of her absence never really goes away. It diminishes sometimes; it ebbs and flows. But it's always hanging around in the background like a gatecrasher. (No, that's too soft an image – it's more like a stalker.)

I've brought with me a large framed photograph of Renee. I had to pack it very carefully lest it get broken in transit; but fortunately it remained in one piece. It shows her at her best: cheerful, happy, at ease. All those characteristics that drew me to her in the first place.

I keep it on my desk so that I can see her whenever I want to. How important it is to see her *face*. It's our faces that reveal – or conceal – who we are. Not that Renee was much good at concealment. The face that looks out at me is the same person who found it almost impossible to wear masks (in the metaphorical sense), a trait that sometimes got her into trouble. Dissembling was not her forte, thank God. It means that the Renee in the photo is real.

When I feel truly sad – which on some days is all the time – I simply caress her face through the glass and gently talk to her. She had such smooth skin, even in death, that the touch of the glass can almost feel like her. When I do this, it doesn't require much to imagine I still have some kind of contact – even physically – with her. And that's comforting because it means that there's still a connection of sorts between us, even if it's only symbolic.

But what I wouldn't give for the real thing.

II

Why is touch so important? A rational onlooker seeing me run my fingers over a glass-covered image of somebody who's died might suppose me unhinged or delusional. If they were of a kindly disposition, they might say they 'understand' in a patronising sort of way.

But the power of touch, even the symbolic touch, has a purity and profundity about it that defies that kind of reaction. This is something I have discovered since Renee lapsed into un-consciousness six days before the end. Not being able to have a conversation with her meant that simple physical gestures came to assume a much greater significance than ever before. They bore the whole weight of our connectedness: the caressing of her forehead, the stroking of her cheek, the holding of her hand – all became pathways to her soul.

I've often wondered what they meant to *her* during that time: whether Renee actually felt the love I was trying to infuse through these little acts of intimacy. In my more doubtful moments, the rationalist in me whispers that they conveyed nothing, that they might have brought comfort to me but not to her.

But Q sent an email over the weekend recalling that on one occasion when she was singing quietly to Renee in her unconscious state, Renee actually squeezed her hand – yes, *squeezed* it. So the doctors were right: although her left brain was unable to communicate, her right brain wasn't.

If only she had squeezed *my* hand. But then I didn't sing to her.

III

It's been an emotional day. Writing my thoughts and feelings down helps to some extent. It gets the thoughts out of my head, where they all too easily keep on colliding with one another and onto paper where they can give voice to the feelings that so readily overpower me.

I suppose one way of looking at it is to see that by putting things into words, I'm achieving a measure of control over the emotional chaos that reigns within. It's not that this removes or avoids the pain. Words can't do that. If they could, more people would become writers instead of drug addicts.

No, the act of writing down, far from distancing me from the truth, makes the reality of Renee's death absolute. There's a starkness about words that can't be avoided. Unlike some lovesick teenager writing a diary to escape a non-existent or broken down love affair, I'm keeping this journal because it keeps on confronting me with the finality of my situation: Renee has gone forever and no mere words can change that. But they can somehow still connect me to her. And for that I'm thankful.

Tuesday 15 April

Widower. It's such a brutal term. Today was the first time I've had to put it in writing. I had to fill in a form to receive dental treatment and the question was: what is your marital status? Answer – tick one of the following boxes: single, married, divorced, widowed. So there it was for all to see in black and white. As if a visit to the dentist wasn't painful enough ...

Wednesday 16 April

P says yes, for which I'm grateful but nervous.

Also, session two with G today. I took my photographs of Renee, expecting to talk about them. But we quickly got onto Renee's last days instead. Heaps of Kleenex. I use so much that I now take my own box.

I mentioned that Q had emailed last week to say that just before Renee went into hospital for the final time, she had confided to Q that she thought we were more in love now than ever. She also told Q that she believed she would never return home. So she knew she was dying. I hadn't known about this conversation and broke down as soon as I read the email.

Then I told G about an awful thought that had occurred to me while driving around Pasadena: namely, that Renee had *voluntarily* given up her life earlier than she might have done in order to spare me further agony. Until Q's email, I hadn't thought of this. But now it begins to make dreadful sense: the hospital doctors said to me shortly before Renee died that, apart from the cancer, she was very robust. Because the cancer was short-lived and aggressive, she hadn't been worn down by months of debilitation (for which she and I were thankful). But, given her robustness and strength of spirit, it's entirely possible she could have struggled for some time longer. The fact that she died when she did, in the manner she did, suggests that *she gave up her spirit* rather than cling on for a few more days or weeks.

If that's true, then Renee chose to die *as an act of love*. I can think of nothing more Christlike. She could have clung to life ('Do not go gentle into that good night'[3]); but instead she lovingly and graciously gave herself into the hands of God at a time of their choosing. Such a thought is stunning: that even on her deathbed she should have loved me that much. I find myself weeping as I write these words.

Needless to say, G had much to say about this. His reflection was that in dying as she did, Renee was choosing to impart a final gift of freedom to me and that I should receive it as such. And when I re-run the end of her life on the projector inside my head, I can see how it all fits. The implications are so tremendous I can only cry at the extent of her love.

Thursday 17 April

Desolation all day. Nothing but a sense of utter emptiness, abandonment and hopelessness. Today is Maundy Thursday, so I shouldn't be surprised. Is this how Gethsemane felt, only worse? If so, how did Jesus bear it?

I'm glad I'm off duty and have no responsibilities at church or anywhere else. The emotions are just too strong. This evening's service of stripping the altar got to me and I found myself weeping copiously as the artifacts were progressively removed until all that was left was a bare table. It felt as if the action perfectly symbolised my life – everything of meaning stripped away until I'm left emotionally naked.

And tomorrow is Good Friday...

[3] The first verse of Dylan Thomas' poem reads: 'Do not go gentle into that good night,/Old age should burn and rave at close of day;/Rage, rage against the dying of the light'. From *The Nation's Favourite Poems* (London: BBC, 1998 edn), p. 63.

Good Friday
Friday 18 April

This is the day I've been dreading. The bleakness and forsaken-ness pictured in the Gospels is a powerful enough story in itself. But it resonates even more with me this year because Renee's death has left me feeling abandoned too. Not that she has *deliberately* deserted me, of course, but the sense of aloneness is as strong as if she had. Compared to the suffering of Christ, mine seems so self-centred and petty. But the pain of Renee's loss is real and this perhaps helps me understand in a small way the humanity of the one who felt an isolation so much greater than mine.

I haven't been through the photo folder for a few days (What does that mean? Surely I'm not caring less about her already?); but I did so again this morning. It brought everything back as I expected (and possibly hoped) it would. The pictures of Renee's grave for the first time evoked a desire actually to be there talking to her, telling her about my thoughts and feelings and chatting to her as if she were still around. Maybe this has some-thing to do with the fact that this will be the first Easter we have not celebrated together since we got married. It's as if being at her graveside would somehow keep the continuity going.

I find myself remembering Easter 2001 in Perth, Australia. It was a glorious day – sunny and warm. Renee was able to get to church with ease and the building was disability-friendly. I'm so glad we had that final trip down under with its photos of Renee in her wheelchair dodging the molestations of an inquisitive emu. Last year (2002), we celebrated it at Winterbourne while David and Leann from Fuller were on sabbatical at Trinity. A nice irony there: twelve months ago, California came to us; now I've gone to California – but without Renee.

Easter Eve
Saturday 19 April

Today is Easter Saturday – that limbo between Good Friday and Easter Day – and I feel as if I'm shut in the tomb. Yesterday was heartbreaking at so many levels. I broke down during one of the hymns at the noonday service that spoke of our being like Christ in the manner of our dying. I, of course, found myself thinking once more of Renee's final gift and even now am indescribably moved at the thought of such love through all those layers of unconsciousness.

It's a double agony today. Not only is there the residue of Gethsemane and Calvary but I also drove into the mountains again. It was glorious weather and there was still one of our favourite places I hadn't visited. The air for once was clear and the terrain outstanding. It seemed more real than ever before. The only trouble was that this was a new reality: Renee wasn't there. I was in the mountains we loved, in the country we loved but without the woman I loved.

The literature says the pain will begin to diminish at some point. But I don't know when. It feels as if my chest will keep on swelling till it bursts, leaving my innards all over the ground. The sheer intensity is almost overwhelming and the temptation to run away into some kind of distraction or diversion is greater than ever before. Maybe this is what being in limbo means.

Easter Day
Sunday 20 April

I was the celebrant at Communion this morning for the first time in months. I could have dropped out but wanted to honour the invitation, especially today of all days. At the sight and sound of a church filled with people declaring that Christ is risen, I had trouble keeping my composure. Fortunately the professional switch inside me flicked on and it was okay.

But how bittersweet! For the person I most wanted to take part in the great affirmation of Easter faith was already enjoying resurrection. It's not only Christmas that is difficult for the bereaved.

Tuesday 22 April

Good third session with G yesterday. Not so agonising as the first or second, maybe because I don't feel quite so desolate, having gathered some who will walk to Gethsemane with me. Of these, P is proving a truly faithful companion who is committed to walking every step of the way and doesn't hesitate to be there when needed. G has encouraged me to see all these people as a gift of God. (In fact, G is so affirmative that I'm not sure whether there's *anything* he wouldn't view as a gift from God.)

At one point our discussion left me reeling. G offered a definition of grief as 'the residue of unfinished emotional agendas'. Unfinished, that is, between the person who has died and the surviving loved one(s). The greater the issues left unresolved, the harder and longer the grief process will be. Nothing blocks grieving like issues that were never dealt with.

I saw this in parish ministry all the time, particularly when sudden deaths occurred: couples who never resolved the fallout from fights they had experienced years ago; rifts that were never healed; love affairs that were never admitted; forgiveness never offered or accepted. How we fool ourselves …

As G and I looked at the residue left behind for Renee and me, the astonishing thing was that there doesn't seem to be any. It wasn't that we had *never* had it; but since the breast cancer in 1998 we determined to keep very short emotional accounts. A brush with death has that sort of effect. I couldn't believe it but the more G and I explored the relationship Renee and I had, the more it became clear that by the grace of God *there is no residue*.

According to G, this means that the grieving process may not be as protracted as I've been fearing. I had been thinking two or three years, as the textbooks say. But to think I might not have to endure the agony for so long holds out real hope. It feels as if my sentence might have an end to it after all. The thought that twelve months might see me through the worst (as G thinks will likely be the case) helps me beyond belief.

But am I just deceiving myself? The cynic that lives on my shoulder like a malign Jiminy Cricket questions whether this can really be true. 'You must be in denial, it's all wishful thinking, there must be *something* left unresolved,' he accuses. 'Nobody has that kind of relationship. Come on, get real! You're hiding something.'

And then I wonder whether I'm hearing from G only what I want to hear. Of course I'm bound to leap at the idea of twelve months rather than twenty-four or thirty-six. Who wouldn't? When you're strapped to the rack, you want the agony over and done with, don't you?

Thursday 24 April

An emotional day yesterday, from which I'm still recovering. The group of students visiting from Trinity[4] went to the Arboretum in the morning, Rodeo Drive and Hollywood in the afternoon and then Chuck and Shelby's house at Pacific Palisades in the evening. I joined them for everything but now wonder whether this was a mistake.

My emotions got more and more raw as I recalled the last time Renee and I visited each of these places. In Hollywood I

---

[4] It so happened that a team of Trinity College students were leading a mission week at St Mark's Church, Altadena. This had been arranged a year before; the plan had been that I would lead the team as part of my sabbatical. In the event, I took a back seat but was more than glad for the team to be there. They proved themselves more than able pastors of their College Principal and I remain grateful to them even now.

had to slope off for a weep in the back streets because people were buying souvenirs for their spouses back home. The evening was perhaps the worst because Renee always used to enjoy (with an almost girlish delight) the view over the Pacific from Chuck and Shelby's patio, especially at night with the whole of LA lit up like a Christmas tree.

C. S. Lewis didn't find his grief intensified by any particular place. But I've found the opposite. I've been systematically visiting – on my own – all the places we used to love going to. I take Renee's favourite teddy bear in the passenger seat of the car (representing Renee) and when we arrive at a place, the bear and I sit for a few minutes.

Then I write an entry in the journal and pray a short prayer of recollection. Every single stop sparks off memories that make me profoundly sad – not so much for the memories themselves which were happy – but for the might-have-beens that will never come true. Maybe it's because Renee and I were married longer; or perhaps it's because she absolutely loved these places.

I must think more about the spirituality of *place*.

Meanwhile the issue of my return to Bristol looms. I've been putting it out of my mind as much as possible. But now I've passed the halfway point, I can't avoid it any longer.

The whole idea fills me with terror. I'm dreading going back to that empty house which carries so many of Renee's imprints without the faintest hope of her ever being there again. I still think of it as the place from which she was taken away to die. I don't belong there (or anywhere else for that matter). I have a house, not a home. My home was where Renee was. Now she's gone, to all intents and purposes I'm homeless.

II

I'm sinking. As the day wears on I feel like I'm going beneath the waves for the second time. Emotionally, I'm so massively exposed on every front that I don't know what or how I should feel. Every feeling that could possibly exist seems to be caught up in a maelstrom inside which just keeps on sucking me down, a whirlpool.

The biggest grief is for the void that Renee leaves. Not only is my wife dead but so is my lover, my best friend, my confidante, my lifelong companion, my emotional rock, my alter ego, my conscience, my spiritual adviser, my *soulmate*.

No wonder I feel abandoned. Have I reached Gethsemane at last? It feels like it.

III

Such waves of despair. I really am going under now. Everything seems pointless and meaningless. I haven't felt anything like this for a week but suddenly I feel completely without hope. It won't go away, no matter what I do.

No doubt this has something to do with visiting yet another reminder this afternoon – the Huntington gardens. Another place Renee loved.

But this time, it seems more than that. It feels as if there is no point to my life except, in the words of the Simon and Garfunkel song, 'continuing to continue'. But why bother? My job can be done perfectly well by somebody else. After all, if I, rather than Renee, had died last month, the process of appointing a new principal would now be in full swing. The kids are independent and self-sustaining; the dog has an alternative home; my friends have their own lives to lead and don't need a grieving widower cluttering everything up.

So it really boils down to this: the one distinctive difference I used to make was caring for Renee. That was the one thing that I – and only I – could do. Now even that's been taken away, what's left?

Never have the despair and sense of abandonment been so deep and all-pervading. Nobody to give love to and nobody to give it back. Is that the definition of hell?

Maybe I'm beginning the slide into clinical depression. That's what the books predict, after all. Up till now I thought I had avoided it by walking into the pain rather than running away from it. Now I'm not so sure. I can see why ending one's life is an awful temptation for some. The prospect of ending the torture must be attractive.

But that's not for me. Even when I'm as sunk in despair as I am today, I know that suicide would be no answer at all. Oh, it might appear to end the pain. But for whom? Certainly not for the people who would be left wondering what they might have done to prevent it and bearing the burden of guilt for having failed. No, it would be a purely selfish act, a negation of the love that others have so clearly shown me and of the love of God made incarnate in them. A betrayal.

I really have reached Gethsemane.

Friday 25 April

Not quite so bleak this morning. It helps that I can pick up the phone and talk to P or that P is willing to make time to meet (an enormous sacrifice, I know, given the busyness of P's schedule). I also find myself looking at the photo album several times a day, as if by doing so I can somehow connect with the life Renee and I had together. It's so very painful but I'm drawn to it by a powerful instinct I can't explain. Sometimes I even half wish I could be back at her graveside just talking to her.

At first, I thought this might be evidence of denial. After all, you hear about people who can't face the fact that their loved one is dead, so they carry on as if nothing has happened or they try to hang onto the past and the things that symbolise it as if somehow this will mean that the dead person is still in their midst.

But the more I think about it, what I'm doing is the opposite of this: a recognition that I face a new reality – life without Renee – which flows out of the past but which is going to be radically different. I don't need persuading she is dead – after all,

I watched her die. But I wish I had some idea of what this new world is going to look like.

I don't feel as pointless and meaningless as I did twenty-four hours ago; but it still feels pretty awful. The cancer has a lot to answer for. It has not only robbed my wife of her life but it has wrecked mine and continues to do so. If ever there were a perfect symbol of evil, cancer surely is it.

Saturday 26 April

Looking back over the week, it's been pretty dreadful. Not exactly Easter faith, full of hope and new life. More like the Passion. Somehow the symbolism seems to be out of synch.

But maybe that doesn't matter. The point about sorrow is that it totally disorders your life to the point where the only constant is chaos. Maybe Easter for me this year symbolises not so much the immediate actuality of joy and rebirth, but rather the promise that it will one day come. A kind of seed lying dormant – all very Pauline.

Sunday 27 April

Eight weeks. Grief specialists say that some kind of turning point often occurs at this stage but I can't tell. Certainly, it doesn't feel any different. Sadness and sorrow are never far from the surface.

I preached on resurrection at this morning's Communion services. My point was that we need to see the resurrection of Jesus not simply as an historical event but as a living truth. It's no good believing that Jesus rose from the dead if this has no impact on our lives here and now. The objective and subjective aspects of belief must come together. Otherwise we're left with either an intellectual affirmation (the objective aspect) or an existential experience not necessarily rooted in fact (the subjective aspect).

There's nothing new in any of this but right now it takes on an extra resonance. The truth of resurrection is what keeps me going: 'She is not here but risen.' I simply can't think otherwise. To do so would make a mockery of all that I believe with my head and feel with my heart. If the dead are not raised, Paul is right: we're wasting our time. God doesn't exist, the incarnation is an illusion, faith is empty, Renee lies rotting in the grave and any sense of connectedness I have with her is no more than a psychological trick, a fantasy.

So the resurrection of Christ isn't just an article of the creed: it's much more than that. It's an existential truth that changes lives and it gives us meaning. But equally, Christian faith without the historical resurrection promises nothing but tears in the end. It's only the raising of Jesus from death that guarantees our own.

But then again, given the week I've just had – especially Thursday – am I being hypocritical in preaching like this? Where was resurrection on Thursday? Or maybe that was the harrowing of hell.

II

A large dose of reality therapy this evening. It was my first social engagement with strangers since Renee's death. I knew it wouldn't be easy but it was even harder than I had thought. I felt her absence like a chill wind, especially as most of the people present were couples. It's not as if I haven't attended plenty of similar occasions on my own in the past – Renee's disability often meant that. But I always knew that she would be at home when I returned. Her presence was a given, a fixed point.

Now it's her *absence* that is the fixture, the axis around which my new world must revolve. She's no longer here and never will be – it's as simple and painful as that. For the past twelve years (since her disability set in), my life has been organised around Renee. But overnight that's disappeared and I'm now completely disoriented. I have no one to consider but myself – and I hate it. Knowing this is what every widow and widower feels doesn't help. I just want her back.

Wouldn't it be wonderful if God were to resurrect everybody right now? But I suppose the earth might get a bit crowded.

Monday 28 April

Met G again today to talk about my re-entry into 'normal' life. We looked at support systems back home and I realised how vulnerable I am. Renee *was* my support. To make it more difficult, the time and energy I had to devote to caring for her meant that I never got much time to develop wider social networks. If I had the past four years all over again, this is the one thing I would do above everything else.

We also talked about the metaphors I feel to characterise my situation. (How keen G is to use them as interpretative keys!) Not surprisingly, they're all negative and solitary. The pain of isolation was evident and the more we looked at it, the more devastating it felt.

There were no quick fixes – there never are. But we did identify some tasks for me to do: I have to develop new, more positive, metaphors; draw up a list of people in the UK who might form a support network; begin to think what changes I might make to the house to reflect 'I' rather than 'I-Thou'.

Although I agreed with these, it all felt a bit clinical, especially as my guts were wanting to scream out: 'Why should I have to go through this? Can I really do it? Can't I just stay here where it's safe?' So the session didn't help much with the pain: my fear of returning is too great. Yet I know I must do it, just as I knew I had to walk the grief journey in the first place. God give me courage.

wednesday 30 April

A dreadful day. I went to the Men's Breakfast run by St Mark's; but although I enjoyed the company and the food, it was over-shadowed by anticipation of the awful job ahead – sorting through the personal possessions that Renee and I left in store at the Fuller Guest Center last summer in readiness for this sabbatical.

There was something brutally final about this. Going through the clothes, books, CDs, tapes and personal possessions that Renee had kept back for our repeated visits to California brought back so many reminders of how much she delighted in being here and her gleeful – almost childlike – anticipation of returning on sabbatical. A number of the items she had bought especially for this time remained unused. As I emptied the case, the memories and hopes all came tumbling out: the blouses and skirts; the summer tops (good for use in California but not back home); the beach robe only ever worn at Paradise Cove; the sandals she wore all the time in the warmth of southern California but not in chilly Britain.

I can't believe I'll never see her in any of these again.

Then there were the personal oils and cosmetics. Renee had always had an unbelievably smooth skin, even to the day of her burial. I'll never forget the touch of her forehead and her hand in the coffin.

Also, the books she purposely left unread: Isaac Asimov, Arthur C. Clarke, Ellis Peters, the Desert Mothers. I remember pushing her around the Pasadena bookshops and the thrill she felt when she discovered them. And then the CDs: the Narnia series, *The Screwtape Letters*, the BBC edition of *The Nation's Favourite Poems*, and, of course, her treasured *Lord of the Rings*.

But the most poignant moment came with the discovery of her teenage Bible (inscribed to Miss Renee Bosworth) in which she had underlined verses about eternal life and God's faithfulness. She had also written in the flyleaf:

> There's only one thing matters
> in this passing world of sin;
> that our lives should tell for Jesus,
> be of some account for him.

Then the words of the *St Patrick's Breastplate* hymn:

> Christ be with me, Christ within me,
> Christ behind me, Christ before me,
> Christ beside me, Christ to win me,
> Christ to comfort and restore me.
> Christ beneath me, Christ above me,
> Christ in quiet, Christ in danger,
> Christ in hearts of all who love me,
> Christ in mouth of friend and stranger.

The power of these words, written in Renee's youthful hand, spoke to me of the strength of faith that characterised not just her latter years but her entire adult life. Reading them out loud and imagining their fulfilment for her in heaven now was just too much to bear. I'm glad P was with me. It was the first time either of us had done this kind of thing. As we sat on the floor, surrounded by the things Renee cherished, passing the Kleenex back and forth, we wept. P will take the clothes to the Salvation Army tomorrow.

More of this kind of thing awaits me, I know, back home (I haven't even unpacked the bags we brought back from hospital the day she died). But at least I've now done it once.

Monday 5 May

I've not journalled since last Wednesday, so it feels a bit odd putting pen to paper again. I feel as if I've become lazy. The few days with Chuck and Shelby in Palm Springs and Pacific Palisades have refreshed me, though once again I think of how much Renee would have enjoyed their company too and my enjoyment is mixed with sadness. Is that the way it will always be?

A and B took me to a dinner party over the weekend where, as the English guest, I found myself seated at the right hand of the hostess. The food was good and the conversation interesting but I was the only single person there and I felt it. It's strange counting the chairs around the table and realising that you're the reason they're arranged as an odd number. The other guests knew about Renee's death and were genuinely kind. One tried to reassure me that I would find someone new with whom to share my life in due course. Her brother had been widowed only eighteen months ago and was getting married again next week. So (she urged) I should not lose heart!

I know people are only trying to comfort me but I'm not ready for this kind of conversation right now. It only reminds me of what I've lost and how much I would give to have Renee back. Her absence still stretches over everything like the sky, even though the grey is a bit more textured and there's an occasional flash of blue. I know it will lighten someday – perhaps sooner than I think – but that day is not yet.

Tuesday 6 May

It's Tuesday again and I hate it. Two months to the day since the funeral. Two months! On one hand it seems as if it were only yesterday that we were lowering Renee into the ground; on the other, so much has happened since then that it might as well be two years. To make it worse, Tuesday was always the day I spent a bit more time with her. When we were in the parish, it was our weekly day off; and since coming to Trinity, it has been my study day spent working at home. Now Tuesdays will always be associated with sorrow.

To add to the turmoil, I received a very touching email today from someone who hardly knows me and who didn't know Renee at all. But we did have a lengthy conversation last November, so I know her a little. But that's not the point. It was the caring tone of her email, from her husband and herself, which moved me. That people who never met Renee and who barely know me should show such compassion moves me to tears. Indifference I can bear: it's love I can't handle.

Then there are the fears that continue to stalk me about returning to Bristol. I've only got one more week here and it feels as if I'm counting the days to my execution. I really don't want to go back. It's an illusion, I know, but California feels a whole lot more like home. In our final counselling session yesterday, G and I named the fears out loud: loneliness, entering an empty house, living with Renee's absent presence, emotional isolation, lack of support, re-entry into the place from which Renee was taken to die.

But oddly, at the same time as I write this, I have an almost inexplicable longing to see her grave again: to stand at her side and talk to her; to tell her of my time here; to remind her that I love her; to seek her advice for the future. So maybe I'm ready to go back after all, no matter how painful it will be.

Monday 12 May
Starbucks, Los Angeles airport

These have been a difficult few days. The successive farewells have taken their toll. I said goodbye to G on Friday (my security blanket now gone?). He reassures me I'm an emotionally healthy guy. But I have to take that on trust. Then there were all the goodbyes at church yesterday. And this morning I bade an emotional farewell to P whose inner strength has kept me going and who has uncomplainingly seen me through so much these last few weeks that I wish I could find some way of adequately showing my gratitude. This either goes to show the attachments

I have developed here or the dread I hold of returning home. Or both.

Travelling to the airport brought the tears once more. Yet another reminder of the journey Renee and I used to make (it's funny how you remember even the smallest details such as the conversations you used to have in the car). One more journey without her, one more reminder of something else that will never be.

Rats! I've been ambushed by grief again. Another eleven hours of this. Will I make it?

Looking around, I find myself surrounded by couples: men and women walking hand-in-hand, sitting patiently (or not so patiently) side by side in the departure lounge, drinking coffee together in Starbucks. And although there are also plenty of single people travelling, they're mostly young. Their joys lie ahead, not behind.

So many memories. At the check-in, of our being fast-tracked because Renee was in a wheelchair. At the security gate, of her being frisked and the chair taken apart in search of drugs; at the departure lounge, of our seemingly interminable waiting followed by pre-boarding on account of her disability.

Then there were the times we were able to get complimentary upgrades. So much of our travel centred on the fact of Renee's disablement. Another reminder of the life I have lost. I'm now the single traveller with no special claims to greater consideration than anybody else. Death is the great leveller in more ways than one.

I wonder if others around me have noticed the tears? It doesn't matter. I gave up thoughts of hiding my grief under a bushel the day I left Britain. In America it's permissible to emote, especially in California. And if it's not okay here and now, then too bad. I have a right to grieve (how American I have become – a *right* to feel ripped apart!)

On the plane

Sitting next to a middle-aged couple who are obviously happy, I look around and force myself not to think of Renee. Every time my guard slips, I think of our flights all over the world – to America, to Asia, to Australia – and her absence elbows its way into every emotional nook and cranny. How much she achieved in these last years, despite everything.

Distraction therapy is only half the answer. There's a limit to the number of hours of movies I can watch. Sandra Bullock and Hugh Grant may be cute, but not endlessly so. Well, not Hugh Grant anyway.

I wonder what all these people are flying back to? Holidays, families, jobs, lovers. Perhaps even illness or tragedy. But whichever, it remains personal to each of them, just as my sorrow is personal to me. In the end we feel our emotions alone. No one else can feel them for us, no matter how empathic they may be.

Except that Christianity holds that God feels them too. God enters into our suffering so that it is never just *ours*. Unless, of course, we believe in a sub-Christian God who is unfeeling or who has nothing to do with his creation. Or unless we dismiss the whole idea of God, in which case postmodern nihilism has the last laugh after all.

But assuming this isn't the case, there's something both comforting and disturbing about the Christian God. To think that the Father created the world and cares for his creation is comforting. But to think also that only through the suffering of his Son could he redeem the world is deeply disturbing. It means that love and suffering are the pattern of life, even the divine life. No wonder early Christians were ridiculed; for what kind of God submits himself to die at the hands of those he has created?

Believing this doesn't remove the pain but it does give perspective for which I'm glad.

Tuesday 13 May
Still on the plane

Okay, so God shares in our pain. But how does he do it? I'm not asking by what *means* he bears our suffering. The Gospel has a clear answer to this: the Son bears our pain and sin in himself on the cross.

No, the question I'm asking is more naive than that: how on earth (or in heaven) can God cope with the sheer quantity of pain that must assail him at any given moment? When we consider the volume of human suffering (we'll leave the animals out of it for now, though their pain is presumably a reality that God bears as well), it becomes impossible to conceive what it must feel like to God to bear all this.

Most of us find it difficult enough to carry *one* person's pain but what about seven billion? And that's only the generation of humanity alive right now. There are also the generations of those who have died since the beginning. How can God bear it all? It's literally unimaginable.

But by faith this is what we believe. I find myself lost in wonder at a God who loves like this.

End of flight

We're about to land at Heathrow and I'm still caught up in the thought that God somehow bears the pain of the whole world, past, present and future. It means he carries *my* pain. So although I'm scared stiff about returning home, that seems minor compared to the suffering of the whole world, or even of other individuals.

As I look back on the past six weeks, my suffering has been real enough and continues to be so. But God has been there in the midst of it and so have others, not least G and P. So maybe God will give me yet more companions for the next stage of the journey. I can't say I'm looking forward to it but I know I'm returning stronger than when I left and that God's graciousness has strengthened me so far, even though I shall continue on an emotional roller coaster. I can't help but think about Renee as I return to Bristol but perhaps the sky is not quite so uniformly grey and low all the time; and perhaps the sun might someday begin to shine after all.

Postscript: December 2003

And you probably don't want to hear tomorrow's
    another day
But I promise you you'll see the sun again
And you're asking me why pain's the only way to
    happiness
And I promise you you'll see the sun again.[5]

[5] Dido, 'See the Sun', from the album *Life for Rent* (2003), Arista Records.

PART THREE

Letters to Alex

Letter 1

Dear Alex,

You were right: making my spiritual journal available for all to read was no easy decision; so I'm thankful that you agreed to read it in advance. As you point out, we've both been through grief: in your case for a sister; in mine, for a spouse. Neither is easy. The death of each removes a part of us that can never be replicated, even though we may 'move on' (as the jargon goes). But maybe we've been the lucky ones. We've known what it means to watch someone die – to embrace them one last time, to impart a farewell kiss at the final dreadful moment and then to give them over to the love of God:

> I will hold the Christ light for you
> in the night time of your fear;
> I will hold my hand out to you,
> speak the peace you long to hear.[1]

So when I look around and see how contemporary society represses all thoughts of death, desperately shielding itself from the reality and horror of its own mortality, I begin to think that, in a strange kind of way, you and I have been fortunate. Death no longer terrorises us through mystery.

But to reach adulthood and never to have experienced the death of a loved one (as is now the case for so many) leaves me wondering how this collective avoidance will ever be broken. For when death happens, as it inevitably does, it hits those who are unprepared like a tsunami. What's more, this is a peculiarly modern phenomenon: our forebears would have been

[1] From the song 'Brother, sister, let me serve you', Richard Gillard, *Sing Glory* (Stowmarket: Kevin Mayhew/Jubilate Hymns, 1999).

astonished to learn that whole generations have no knowledge of this most basic of human experiences and consequently don't know how to grieve when the reality is thrust upon them. The same forebears would have been equally shocked to find that grieving has become a completely individualistic experience – a pain to be endured alone in the solitariness of one's soul, behind locked doors, away from the world. (Grief, after all, remains a contagious disease!) Death is barely acknowledged, except by immediate friends and neighbours. Otherwise, it's assumed to be a personal (i.e. individual) matter, in which the griever is to be left in their private world to come to terms with their catastrophe in the aloneness of abandonment. Cartesian philosophy with its reduction of personhood to the introspective thinking self has a lot to answer for.

But back to your question: what has *my* grief been like? At gut level, I can give a straightforward answer: it's been hellish. There's nothing like it. Day after day it relentlessly bears down upon you, ripping your psyche apart as it destroys everything in its path, tearing up your life until all that's left is a pile of shreds waiting to be vacuumed up or blown away. Of all the primary emotions we experience, grief is the most merciless: it remains wholly without pity. Spike Milligan's poem 'Oberon' captures it exactly:

> The flowers in my garden
> > grow down.
> Their colour is pain
> Their fragrance sorrow.
> Into my eyes grow their roots
> > feeling for tears
> To nourish the black
> > hopeless rose
> > within me.[2]

[2] Spike Milligan, *Small Dreams of a Scorpion* (Harmondsworth: Penguin, 1973), p. 38. Reproduced by permission of Spike Milligan Productions Ltd.

But you want to know about more than my guts. This is diffi-cult since much of the last ten months has been dominated by them, albeit in changing ways. In my more reflective moments, though, it seems to me that grief can be characterised by a number of metaphors.

I wish I could say they weren't predominantly negative. But to do so would be to play a game of make-believe for the sake of avoiding the harsh reality: grief is soul-destroying. So I'm not going to pull any punches, even though I would say that the pas-sage of time does make a difference. The further I get from Renee's death, the less harsh the metaphors become. They no longer dominate in the way they used to. They can be just as intense – but for much shorter periods.

Perhaps the kindest one I can think of is that of the gate-crasher. I've lost count of the number of times grief has turned up uninvited and unannounced and then proceeded to demand admission. And as with most gatecrashers, it's incredibly persistent.

On a good day, I can say no and tell it to go away. But – and this was the case particularly in the early months – it slips in anyway. And once inside, it circulates around the entire room, as it were, infecting every part and every conversation.

However, at least the gatecrasher is mischievous rather than aggressive; unwanted but not necessarily malevolent. Other, more shocking, metaphors also spring to mind. These are the ones that characterised my experience in those first months. And I hesitate even to mention them. But what kind of answer to your question would I be giving if I bowdlerised the fact that it has been the violent metaphors that have so often best expressed grief's reality?

1. *The stalker.* I notice you picked up on this image when you came across it in my journal. You're correct, of course, that the essence of stalking is terror by stealth rather than physi-cally violent intent. But even so, the effect is the same: to exert raw power over the victim until they find themselves

defenceless and unable to resist. So the metaphor points to a simple but important truth: grief delights in creeping up unawares and waiting till the time is ripe. Then it pounces. Once it has achieved this, it has a clear run to do whatever it wants.

2. *The assailant.* I've lost count of the number of times I've come away from a bout of grief feeling as if my guts have been kicked in. Perhaps there's no other way; but I wish there were. The sheer agony of feeling your loved one's absence – in the sure and certain knowledge that it will be permanent – leaves you empty and hopeless. There's nothing to compare with it for sheer unwonted cruelty. Grief is the Nazi of all emotions.

3. *The rapist.* What do I say about this, the most shocking and brutal of all my metaphors? I hardly dare mention it. But the plain truth is that for about four months I felt my emotions *had* been raped. For grieving bears all the hallmarks of this most demonic of acts: invasion of the self's integrity, violation of one's personality, the infliction of brute force, the drive to overpower and subjugate, ruthlessness of purpose, callous disregard for the victim, pitiless exertion of the will-to-power. And, as with rape, the victim of grief is left a wreck stumbling around an emotional wasteland, desolate and destroyed. It's a shocking and frightful image.

You must by now be wondering what state my psyche is in. To be honest, there are times when I've asked myself the same question. So I've tried to come up with other metaphors not so violent:

1. *The seducer/seductress.* I alluded to this in the journal but let me say a little more. In that period of mourning when your whole life seems to have imploded and you are at your wit's end, your beloved may have gone but grief stands ready to offer companionship and comfort of sorts. 'I'll walk by your side through what lies ahead,' it murmurs. 'Don't worry, I'll never leave you. I'll be here as long as you want me.' So, by

some kind of perverted paradox, grief offers to fill the gap created by love departed. By promising constancy, it offers a bizarre new feeling of security that says, 'I will never leave you or forsake you.' The only problem is that all it can offer is a constancy of pain.

I have to admit that more than once I've felt the power of this seduction. It was particularly alluring when all I could feel was the agony of separation and loss. How tempting under those circumstances to listen to grief's whispers, especially when associated with particular remembrances of Renee! It was as if grief offered some kind of Faustian bargain: I could have the pleasure of the memories but only at the price of accepting the pain. 'You can walk with your wife as long as I walk alongside you,' it seemed to say. Even now the seductress occasionally murmurs with success.

2 . *Gravitational pull.* All the other metaphors have been personalistic. This one is different. The point is that just as gravity is irresistible, so is grief. No matter how much you might try to avoid its force, it pulls you toward itself in the end. The only question is whether you end up crashing into the ground or whether you can make some kind of soft landing. All I can say is that I have known both.

A variation on this theme would be to see grief as a black hole – I hope I've got the physics right. As I understand it, a black hole is an area of space-time with such immense gravitational power that it sucks in and crushes everything around it. Even light can't escape the intensity of its pull (hence the term).

This is what makes it such a perfect metaphor. At my worst times, it has felt as if this is exactly what has happened: every bit of my life drawn in and crushed, except the pain of loss. That remains intact. Can you begin to imagine what it's like? (Of course you can – you've known it yourself.) Going to bed in tears and waking up the same; finding yourself at an act of public worship suddenly weeping and desperately trying not to draw attention to your state; spending every hour of the day wishing the misery would recede; wandering around just longing that your beloved would return, even though you know she won't. The black hole sucks everything in until all light is extinguished and darkness becomes the only reality.

Oh dear. As I re-read what I've written, I realise how dismal it all must sound. But I'm afraid you did ask what grief is like. Maybe my letters in future should come with a health warning: 'Beware – reading this could seriously damage your spirits.' I'll try to do better next time. For now, keep on praying.

Francis

Letter 2

Dear Alex,

So you found the metaphors disturbing? I don't know whether to feel sorry or glad. It sounds glib to say that there are times when we *ought* to be disturbed; but the more I've thought about it, the more I've come to the conclusion that's what good metaphors do. That's their purpose. Nonetheless, you're right to point out that grief is as much about process as it is about particular feelings and that there must be some less jarring metaphors to describe the grief *process*.

I guess the image of the journey that I've used is the one that most appeals. Certainly, it's a recurring metaphor throughout the literature.

But what kind of journey? That's the question. Here we enter the territory of grief theory. (By the way, I don't share the all-too-common disdain for 'theory' in opposition to 'practice'. All practice is theory-laden when you examine it carefully, just as all theories lead to practice when you reflect on them.)

The idea of a journey is helpful because it gets us away from the idea that grief is static. Believe me, it's not. The griever is constantly on the move – sometimes forwards, frequently backwards and more often than not going round in circles. The journey is not so much a logistical exercise in getting from one place to another as a re-run of the wandering of the Israelites in the desert. A comment by Althea Pearson seems to me to sum it up well:

> The road is not straight, but winds and curves and doubles back on itself ... The journey can encompass rocky terrain which is arduous and costly to traverse, but may also include some clearings and even some stretches which feel like desert. And the road certainly does not take the

shortest route … but includes hairpin bends as well as relatively straightforward stretches.' [3]

Yet, as I've found, there are dangers in this metaphor. Early grief theorists found themselves hooked on a rigid theory of grief stages which the sufferer is required to go through before he or she can reach the end of the road. These stages were supposed to be fixed and unchanging: the griever had to experience them one by one in a particular sequence; and only when he or she had done so, could they be reckoned to have completed the journey.

I suspect that those who held (or hold) to such a theory have never really thought through what this does to the mourner. I wonder how many theorists have ever grieved? For, as I've found all too readily, adherence to a rigid stage theory imposes on the griever the role of a passive victim: you simply wait for whatever the next stage will throw up, resigned to each one in turn, believing that you have no choice but to submit. It's like being a passenger on a train with no option but to sit in your seat, relentlessly passing through the stations one by one. *Everything* is outside your control: the speed; the experience you can expect at each stop; what will await you along the way. And although you know you'll reach your destination eventually, all you can do is to wait meekly. It's a journey of grim endurance.

Now, I have to say I'm deeply ambivalent about this view. I don't say it has no value at all, for there clearly are different aspects of the grief process that are common to us all. But there's something in me that rebels against the idea of a rigid series of invariant stages over which we are impotent. In my heart of hearts, I find it anathema to think that grieving is just a matter of sticking it out in the desperate hope that things somehow will get better: hanging on as each stage is passed through. It seems so deeply disempowering. But then that's my guts speaking again.

[3] Althea Pearson, *Growing Through Loss and Grief* (London: HarperCollins, 1994), p. 8.

When I apply my head to the issue, I can see that there's merit in knowing that the journey isn't random and that it has definable characteristics. I don't have any problem with that. It's the hard determinism I reject: the view that we're completely at the mercy of forces outside our control. Theologically, we are made for freedom – not in the sense of being without constraints, but in the sense of possessing, under God, a measure of self-determination and choice. The opening chapters of Genesis, after all, portray human beings as created in the image of a God whose nature is perfect freedom. That we've messed it up by our misuse of the gift doesn't devalue its importance. Nor does it rule out that to some degree, we still possess it; or that God intends us to use it for his purposes and glory. But that's precisely what stage theory (in its hard form) does.

Then there's the question of power. Rigid stage theories rob people of power because they deny that we can be *active* in the grief process. Our role is to play the victim with as much good grace as we can muster. Because we're not in the driving seat, we must subject ourselves to the who- or what- ever *is* (in this case, the contingencies that are associated with each stage of the process).

But look what this does to our humanity. It removes from us any significant say in our lives at the very moment we most need it. Just as the griever finds himself facing the monumental task of rebuilding his life from amidst a pile of rubble, stage theories come along and say, 'Sorry – you can't take control yet. You're not up to it. You must go through the following process before you can be regarded as recovered.' Or to revert to the railway metaphor: 'Stay in your seat until the conductor says you can get up.'

On pragmatic grounds alone, this is a counsel of despair; for nothing diminishes hope like disempowerment: just ask any prisoner. It's been frustrating knowing this, only to be faced with stage theories running through grief literature and the medical profession.

You can imagine, then, how I felt when I came across the work of the American grief researcher and therapist Robert Neimeyer. He articulates professionally what I have intuitively sensed: that the counselling and medical professions perpetuate the view – often uncritically – that grief, in his words, is a matter of moving through 'a determined sequence of psycho-logical states' and that 'deviations from such a course are to be considered "abnormal" or "pathological".'[4]

If you think I'm overreacting, let me tell you about a doctor I saw about three months after Renee's death. On hearing that I was sleeping badly, he told me that this wasn't at all surprising at this stage; that I was grieving healthily because I was moving through the stages; and that if I could just tough it out, I would find the next stage easier in a few weeks' time. In a year or so – maybe two – I would have recovered once I had got through the process. In the meantime, did I want any anti-depressants?

But, leaving aside the pragmatics, there are at least two other theological reasons why I'm doubtful about stage theories, at least in their 'hard' form. The first goes back to the issue of power. If God is a God who offers us the gift of freedom, does he not also offer us the gift of empowerment? Surely this is what it means to be made in his image? If, as the Genesis passages suggest, we're created to be the vice-rulers over his creation, doesn't this imply that he gives us authority – and by implication, power – to do so?

Now I'm well aware that humanity has abused this gift. But the inbuilt capacity for moral awareness and responsibility given to the first humans in the Genesis story remains, despite the intrusion of sin and the inborn sinfulness that has flowed from the disobedience of our first parents. We continue to be morally responsible beings. This is the essence of being made in God's image. Our moral will has been corrupted; but this is where doctrines of redemption and the kingdom of God come in.

[4] Robert A. Neimeyer, *Lessons of Loss: A Guide to Coping* (Memphis, Tennessee: Center for the Study of Loss and Transition, 1998), pp. 84–5.

All this is a somewhat discursive way of saying that a *biblical* view of what it means to be human must lead us to a *radical* view of freedom and empowerment. We can't get away from it.

But there's an even more fundamental reason for my scepticism. Like all determinisms, stage theories appear to leave no room for God. The process grinds on irrespectively. The griever is merely another cog in the machine and God remains *deus ex machina*. He's outside the box.

Yet surely this is a theological point we cannot afford to concede. If we believe in a God who is active in his world, rather than a deity who has wound things up like clockwork and left them to run while he goes off for a cigarette break, we must also believe in a God whose grace is truly active in the midst of pain. The grief process, like any human process, must be open to the work of God's Spirit, the same Spirit whom Jesus calls Comforter. We can have no truck with a God held captive by impersonal processes and forces, no matter how reasonably they might describe what appears to be going on. If I thought that, I would have given up a long time ago.

Put another way, as pastors and theologians, you and I must resist the idea that our pastoral care is nothing but therapy with a religious veneer. Or, to express it more grandly, that it is simply a matter of holding to a different system of symbols and beliefs. No, we must insist on the very thing that makes Christian pastoral care distinctive: faith in the continuous work of the sustaining, renewing and transforming Spirit; a God who is involved with, and who acts upon, natural processes; a God who comes to meet us in love rather than an absentee landlord. This surely throws into question all expressions of determinism, including hard versions of grief stage theory.

So where does that leave us? Or more personally, where does it leave *me*? If I'm not a passive victim subject to forces outside my control, what am I?

If you'll forgive a last bit of philosophy, I think that this is not a question that can be resolved by empirical observation. Or to put it differently, how you interpret the empirical data (watching how grievers deal with their grief) will depend upon the philosophical and theological assumptions you bring to the observations in the first place. We had this debate, if you remember, eighteen months ago when discussing your client who was finding it hard to break free of depression: was she a passive victim of her brain chemistry or was she choosing to stay in depression as the only 'safe' place to be? If I remember rightly, you felt that although the chemical hypothesis was relevant, she was, in fact, making a deliberate choice in favour of depression, odd though that might seem.

Well, the grief issues are identical: passive surrender or active – albeit impaired – choice? Until the last year, I hadn't made the connection. But looking back, I can see how important the choice of explanation is. Interestingly, Neimeyer adopts what he calls 'a constructionist perspective', by which he means that although there are common challenges that face the bereaved to reorientate and reintegrate their lives, there's little evidence for sequential stages that are universal and invariant. Each person does it differently within different timescales and different cultures.

You have no idea what a relief it was for me to come across this insight. My own journey has seemed to sit very loosely with any fixed model at all. I've found that reactions that were supposed to happen in one stage were happening in another and for lengths of time that simply didn't accord with the theories. What am I to make of the fact, for example, that I'm supposed to have no energy and to be unable to reorganise my life at this stage of grieving, yet here I am – writing this book? Or that two months ago, as you know from our email correspondence, I should have been at the peak of energy and reorganisation; yet it felt as if I was in an unending tunnel, scarcely able to get through a week without prolonged periods of darkness and tears.

So I'm with Neimeyer: grieving should be seen as a matter of being empowered to construct new meaning in life, to bring order into chaos rather than to be a passive victim. Or, to use fashionable pastoral language, grief offers the possibility of constructing a new personal narrative out of the collapse of the old. But it's a narrative that the griever *chooses* to construct, however much its components are thrust upon him (or her). The story can be written in multiple ways, with multiple possibilities for it to unfold. There is no predetermined plotline. The bereaved must decide.

But – and here's the rub – the burden of deciding isn't easy. It doesn't remove the pain. When I first realised that I had an active part to play in the grief process, it was as if a prison door sprang open. The sense of regaining power over my own life was overwhelming. But the day-to-day reality of struggle and tears has remained. The feelings of loss and all that goes with it don't go away. If anything, they intensify as you come to grasp that a new reality requires a new way of thinking and living; and that it's up to you to begin the task of reconstruction. Bereavement may be a 'choiceless event' but grieving is not.

So much for the theory: no doubt you'll want to comment on what all this means in practice. Let me steal a march on you by saying that, at the very least, it will mean pastoral carers like you and me will have to regard ourselves as those whose task is to empower as much as to comfort. But then isn't that what our Lord did?

Shalom always,

Francis

Letter 3

Dear Alex,

As usual, you've seen past my avoidance tactics. For all my talk of emotional openness, what about the emotion that hasn't surfaced yet in any of our exchanges: the one that doesn't merely destroy the griever but can lay waste everyone else as well? I mean anger, of course: the emotion on which St Paul instructs us never to let the sun go down. I wonder if he reminded himself of that while writing to the Galatians that his opponents should castrate themselves?

Anyhow, that's not the point. You wonder what I've done with the anger that grievers inevitably feel. Good question; and my silence on the subject perhaps begins to give you an idea. But the answer's complicated, so I'm afraid you're going to have to bear with me.

When Renee was first diagnosed, and then as she rapidly declined, I felt anger towards other people, particularly the doctor who I believed should have spotted the cancer more quickly and got her into hospital a month earlier (I'm not saying now that he *could* have done so – simply that I thought so at the time). I was also pretty angry towards the hospital laboratory that failed to get a clear result on the early tests, thereby leaving the specialists unsure of how to treat her. Both reactions, I now understand, are common. Significantly, I never felt anger towards the medical staff on the hospital ward who cared for Renee day by day.

Once she had died, however, the anger focused on something else: the cancer itself. What was this *thing*, this evil, that had taken Renee's life and ravaged mine – not to mention the lives of our three children? I hated it with all the hate I could muster. Melville's line from *Moby Dick* comes to mind:

And he piled upon the whale's white hump the sum of all the rage and hate felt by his soul always. If his chest had been a cannon he would have shot his heart upon it.

And God? Did I rage against him? The answer is 'No', at least for the first few months. Remember, as a young believer I was brought up to think of anger as sinful; so how could I ever get angry against God? The thought was unacceptable. And although intellectually I haven't held this view for some years, emotionally I realise it has been as strong as ever all along. It wasn't until I watched an episode of *The West Wing* (a drama series about a fictional President of the United States) a few months ago that the suppressed anger broke to the surface. Let me explain.

The episode in question centred on President Bartlet, a devout Roman Catholic, grieving over the death of his secretary, an old family friend killed in a car accident. Angrily he confronts God in the cathedral after her funeral service and vents his rage at God's capriciousness:

> You're a son of a bitch, you know that? She bought her first new car and you hit her with a drunk driver. What – was that supposed to be funny? 'You can't conceive, and nor can I, the appalling strangeness of the mercy of God', says Graham Greene. I know whose ass he was kissing there, 'cos I think you're just vindictive.

He then goes on to remind God of the near murder of one of his aides in an assassination attempt and to accuse God of cruelty in manipulating the forces of nature to bring about death on a grand scale:

> What was Josh Lyman – a warning shot? That was my son: what did I ever do to yours but praise his glory and praise his name?
>
> There's a tropical storm that's gaining speed and power. They say we haven't had a storm this bad since you took

out that tender ship of mine in the North Atlantic last year –
68 crew. You know what a tender ship does? It fixes the
other ships. It doesn't even carry guns – just goes around
and fixes the other ships and delivers the mail: that's all it
can do …

'Thank you God.' Yes I lie. It was a sin. I've committed
many sins. Have I displeased you, you feckless thug? 3.8
million new jobs – that wasn't good? Bailed out Mexico,
increased foreign trade; 30 million new acres of land for
conservation; we're not fighting a war; I've raised three
children. That's not enough to buy me out of the doghouse?

And, as a final gesture of defiance, the President walks to the
centre of the church, lights a cigarette, inhales once and stamps
it out on the beautiful marble floor. God stands accused and his
house desecrated.

My description, of course, completely fails to do justice to the
power of the scene. You have to see it to feel the impact. But,
like all good drama, it spoke *to* me and *for* me. Bartlet felt as I
felt. His feelings echoed mine. Even now I find it hard to watch
the episode without emotion.

But ever since seeing it, I've wondered what I would have
said if the scene had been mine: if I had been the one shouting
at God.

Okay, Renee's gone. She's with you. Are you glad? Does it
please you that the rest of us have to pay the price? *You*
don't. You can just sit there watching over the universe, not
caring what happens, presiding over death and destruction,
maybe even ordering it – after all, it must get pretty bor-
ing sitting on that throne all day being worshipped by all
those boot-lickers. You're the One who said even Cyrus
was his servant, remember? And look what *he* did. But
we're the ones whose lives have been ripped apart. We're
the ones whose hearts are broken, not you. Or doesn't that
matter? I guess not.

Just like it didn't matter to you when Renee got disabled in the prime of life. Just like it didn't matter when she spent two years – two *years* – in agony, no one able to relieve it, no one able to take it away. Where were you when she was bedbound for months on end or when we begged you for help? Anything would have done, however temporary. You didn't care. You just let her – us – go through it without so much as a nod or a wink.

So what kind of God are you? Not exactly a regular guy. Oh, I know all the answers theologians give. There's not one I haven't used in the classroom: omniscient, omnipotent, omnipresent, transcendent, immanent, eternal. Why, you're everything we need.

Bull.

Even worse, you're supposed to be all-loving. Don't make me sick. Augustine got it right when he asked how we could reconcile a God who's all-powerful and all-loving with the kind of godless world we live in. If you loved Renee (and your love was supposed to be so much greater than mine, remember) and if you have the power to create worlds, why didn't you act, why did she die? Why no miracle of healing? It would have been such a small thing for such a great God.

After all, it's not as if I didn't make you an offer at the time: six months longer for her and you would get me for the rest of my life, lock, stock and barrel, no questions asked. But that wasn't enough, was it? You granted Abraham's plea when he begged for Sodom. Why not mine? Six months! It wasn't much to ask for. No more than the blink of an eye. You wouldn't even grant that. What are you – some kind of cosmic sadist?

And what had she done, anyway, to deserve such an end? She gave her life to you when she was a teenager; she worked for the poor in the Third World; she served your church for I don't know how many years; she – we –

adopted three kids; wasn't all that enough? Oh I know we all have to die sometime. Death is our fate. But why now? Why in this way? Do you actually give a toss?

You know, she loved to pray and praise you for hours on end. She had this routine: she'd watch the world news on TV first thing in the morning after I'd left for work, then she'd come downstairs and intercede for the situations she'd just seen. And that would lead to thanksgiving for your goodness and more intercession for people she knew, for college, for anyone who'd asked her. If I phoned during this time, woe betide me. Her life was centred on prayer.

So if hearing people pray is such a delight to your ears, why did you stop her? Were you getting fed up? Did her prayers displease you? Or was it just that you had finished playing with her like a cat with a mouse? 'Game over, time's up.'

'*J'accuse, mon Dieu.*' But I already know what you're going to say. You're going to plead the free will defence. Our first parents, good old Adam and Eve, couldn't keep their hands off the forbidden fruit. They listened to the snake and in came original sin. Creation was busted and nothing's worked right since.

But why didn't you stop them? Answer: because of free will. Why didn't you create them (and us) differently, so that we would choose *you* rather than sin? Answer: because that would have made you into a puppet master. Human beings programmed to love and obey would hardly be loving and certainly not free. Genuine freedom requires the ability to choose evil as well as good. Here's Augustine again, riding to God's rescue.

But if freedom is so important, why is it that you – the perfectly free Being – can never choose evil? Answer: it would be against your character, a contradiction in terms. But doesn't this mean that freedom – in this case *your* freedom – can be reconciled with being able to choose only the good after all? And if that's the case for you, why not for Adam and Eve or for us? I don't get it. It doesn't add up.

You see, the world would have been spared so much suffering if only you had worked to a different design spec. No history of wars, no crusades, no genocides, no holocaust. No babies thrown alive into molten human fat streaming from incinerators next to the gas chambers, no killing fields, no Rwanda, no Vietnam. Nothing.

And Renee would still be alive.

But you don't have an answer, do you? You never do, other than to say, 'Don't ask!' Your mouthpieces, the theologians and teachers of religion, tell us: 'Don't question the mysterious ways of God; who are we to comprehend the plans of the Almighty?' Remember, I'm one of these guys so I know how it works: whenever God's in trouble, invoke his mystery. That'll get him off the hook. There's no answer to it. Perfect.

Well, all I can say is: I hope that satisfies you, 'cos it sure as hell doesn't satisfy me.

Any more than does that other refuge: prayer. 'Ask and it shall be granted unto you, seek and ye shall find, knock and it will be opened' (Matthew 7:7). How many times have I heard (and preached) that?

But you can't lose on this one either, can you? If we pray for something and it happens, we say: 'Hurrah. Praise God for answering prayer.' If it doesn't happen, we say: 'Thank God for knowing better than we do. Praise him for his goodness.'

So nothing, absolutely nothing, can ever count against you, can it? I pray for Renee to live and she does. Hallelujah! I pray the same prayer and she dies: I'm still supposed to shout: 'Hallelujah, God knows best.' What kind of game is that? You've got it all sewn up. Nobody but you can score a point.

Is there anything you can say in your defence, God? Is there any way I can be saved from my cynicism? Or must I stamp out my cigarette and walk? When you're ready, let me know.

Your obedient servant,
Francis

Letter 4

Dear Alex,

I notice you've taken seriously both Bartlet's accusations and mine. Well, the anger you wanted to know about is all there, though I can see you're worried I might have gone too far. Accusing God is not normally in the job description for the principal of a theological college. We're usually expected to be less than human. But isn't it far better to have anger honestly articulated and out in the open rather than hidden behind closed doors? I'm pretty sure you think this: otherwise why would you have been so concerned that I hadn't voiced it? Besides, we both know it's basic counselling technique to give vent to the voice within.

The only problem is: once I've let God have it with both barrels, what do I say to him next?

There was a time I would have thought that only a grovelling repentance would do: that God would not be satisfied with anything less. But now I'm not so sure. You only have to read the Psalms to see how God is used to this kind of thing. He knows our anger isn't trivial and he knows it's a sign of our humanity. Although I'm not proud of myself for the anger, I wonder what God would rather have – repressed feelings of rage overlain by pious doublespeak or an honest confession of reality. However, you can rest easy: I've made my peace with him; and, yes, I did say sorry.

But there's a deeper point: that we need to recognise the kind of questions Bartlet and I were voicing for what they are: pain packaged as philosophical critique: an arsenal of verbal weapons waiting to be discharged for cathartic effect.

So how should I deal with them? One option would be to ignore them, to write them off as mere rantings: 'Lord it was just an emotional tirade. I didn't mean it. It's not worth bothering about.' The difficulty is that I did mean them; they weren't just verbal fireworks. I felt every word. And they do matter – there were serious arguments tucked away somewhere that demand a response. The issue is: what kind of response?

This is where Christian apologetics comes in. Questions about the problem of evil, the purpose of prayer and the nature of God are first-order issues. They are fundamental to our core beliefs. What we believe about these things will determine the kind of lives we lead and how we react when crises envelop us. Just as importantly, our beliefs will colour how we're perceived by others, particularly those who are searching for faith in a confused and bewildered world. So you see, we're not playing games: we're being serious in the search for truth.

But when we've done the apologetic task, we still have more to do. Underneath the intellectual layer lies another, more powerful, one: the emotional–existential. Unless we enable people to deal with this, we shall leave them with tidy intellectual answers but few emotional resources.

Gabriel Marcel once commented that there were two types of people when it came to tackling complicated issues: those who saw them as problems to be solved and those who regarded them as mysteries to be discerned. Marcel viewed this split as the product of Enlightenment thinking, the belief that everything is ultimately explicable by the use of human reason: that if we hammer away hard and long enough at something, we'll be able to crack it, 'as if one were always examining some detached state of affairs which could be coldly dissected and systematically analyzed so as to produce complete and comprehensive knowledge.'[5] When I think about it, this is what most apologetics are; and this is what I have been up to.

But does such an approach actually settle issues where it really counts – in the guts? I suspect not; because they're not just

5 Quoted in Thomas G. Weinandy, *Does God Suffer?* (Edinburgh: T&T Clark, 2000), p. 31.

problems or puzzles. They're fundamental mysteries.

'Aha,' I hear you say. 'You've been forced back upon the very tactic you laid into with such force a week ago: when all else fails, take refuge in mystery.' But it's at this point that we need to revisit Marcel: 'Some fields of human enquiry,' he observes, 'cannot be properly understood, and in actual fact they become distorted, when approached as problems. Rather they must be approached under the rubric of *mystery*.'[6]

In other words, there are some things – human beings, for example, or the nature of God – which, by definition, are beyond problem-solving. They are simply too complicated and irreducible. No matter how much we might investigate and say about them, there is always more to be said. There's no complete explanation or final answer. 'We may come to a greater understanding of human life, but we never come to a complete comprehension of it … The mystery, by the necessity of its subject matter, remains.'[7]

A metaphor may help. The notion of problem or puzzle is perhaps best characterised by the modern detective story. The hero – Sherlock Holmes, Miss Marple, Inspector Morse – relentlessly applies deductive logic to the situation until, step by step, the solution is found. QED. This is Enlightenment thinking translated into popular culture.

But mystery (a misnomer, by the way, when applied to detective stories) can be likened to a spring. We thirst for understanding and explanation but the more we drink, the more we realise that although our thirst is quenched for a time, it will never be satisfied. There is always more to be had. In the words of Jacques Maritain, 'I still thirst and continue to thirst for the same thing, the same reality which at once satisfies and increases my desire. Thus I never cease quenching my thirst from the same spring of water which is ever fresh and yet I always thirst for it.' [8]

6 Ibid.
7 Ibid.
8 Ibid., note 9.

Now as long as we categorise God and human life as problems to be solved, we shall (a) never find satisfactory solutions; because (b) we misunderstand their true nature. We must therefore see them as mysteries instead. This doesn't mean we shouldn't think about them or ask searching questions. Nor does it diminish the role of intellectual inquiry. But once we have made the paradigm switch from problem to mystery, we shall see that the primary aim of theology is not the solution of problems but the 'discernment of what the mystery of faith is.'[9]

So where does that leave President Bartlet, and myself? Traditionally the kind of challenges thrown down by both of us have been met with attempts to defend God by philosophical argument. The free will defence is an obvious example. But I don't think this can any longer be regarded as adequate. It may be necessary to the task but it's not sufficient. Traditional theodicies (justifications of God) will always leave us wanting.

Frustratingly for both of us, I must go now. The pressure of teaching this term requires me to produce a lecture by tomorrow. And I've already been preoccupied this week with the usual run of college business. But stay cool – I'll return to this theme next week.

In the meantime, keep the faith,

Francis

---

[9] Ibid., p. 32. Weinandy goes on to say: 'Because God, who can never be fully comprehended, lies at the heart of all theological enquiry, theology by its nature is not a problem-solving enterprise but rather a mystery discerning enterprise.'

Letter 5

Dear Alex,

I'm sorry I left my thoughts in mid-air last time. Yes, I do want to affirm intellectual defences of the Faith but why are you so concerned to get God off the hook? The fact is that suffering and evil do exist and that the Christian Faith claims that God is at the same time loving and sovereign over all he has made. Paul says it clearly: Jesus is Lord. I can see why you think God needs rescuing. But that's to slip back into the problem-solving approach. Suppose we ask another question: what do we make of the suffering of Christ? He was, after all, God's Son.

By reframing the question in this way, we find ourselves in different terrain. Instead of trying to get God off the hook, we impale him firmly on the cross – which is where he should be. In other words, the key to the mystery is not theodicy (at least not by itself) but Christ. Alongside my cry of 'Why Renee?' must be juxtaposed the cry of another: 'My God, my God, why have you forsaken me?' Two cries of dereliction: one God called upon to answer both.

But does he answer? At first sight, no. He stays silent. The Son suffers and dies while the Father looks on. Is the Father indifferent? That's how it appears but surely it can't be. And so we begin to discern a clue to the mystery of our own suffering. The dying Jesus cries out and God apparently does nothing. That's the way it feels so often when *we* suffer. But wait – he does do something: he enters into the dereliction of the Son so that the suffering of the Son becomes the suffering of the Father and is thereby taken into the life of the Triune Godhead. Jürgen Moltmann puts it like this: 'The abandonment on the cross which separates the Son from the Father is something which takes place within God himself.'[10] And again, 'In the Passion of

[10] Jürgen Moltmann, *The Crucified God* (London: SCM, 1974), pp. 151–2.

the Son, death comes upon God himself, and the Father suffers the death of his Son in his love for forsaken man.'[11]

So the Father does suffer after all. But it's not the suffering of the passive onlooker: rather, it's the suffering of identification. The Father is at one with his Son on the Cross. In Galot's words, 'In the suffering face of the Savior we must also see the suffering face of the Father. Jesus' human suffering enables us to enter into the mystery of the Father's divine suffering.'[12]

What's more, since Jesus is the Son of Man as well as the Son of God, it is the suffering of humanity that is represented and experienced on the Cross. Jesus is the representative human being, the second Adam. Although he dies that we might be forgiven, he bears not just our sin but our suffering as well. And because both Father and Son experience the pain of separation and loss, the death of Christ is a Trinitarian event. Here's Moltmann again:

> What happens on Golgotha reaches into the very depths of the Godhead and therefore puts its impress on the Trinitarian life of God in eternity. In Christian faith, the cross is always at the centre of the Trinity, for the cross reveals the heart of the triune God, which beats for his whole creation.[13]

This is heavy duty theology, I realise. But suffering is a heavy duty subject – no, it's a heavy duty *experience*. The point I'm trying to make is that in the midst of our pain, only a suffering God can help. The God of the philosophers won't do. We need a God who knows what it means to be in pain, not by observing dispassionately but by experiencing it for himself. This is why the incarnation is crucial. The mystery of why we suffer can only be met by the mystery of why the incarnate God suffers.

[11] Ibid., p. 192.
[12] Ibid. Quoted in Weinandy, *Does God Suffer?*, p. 18.
[13] Ibid., note 52.

And the answer to that lies in yet another mystery – that of incarnate love. 'The Father suffers the death of the Son in his love for forsaken man.'

If we come to the cross, then, with the question: '*Why* do we suffer,' we shall be disappointed. But if we approach it with the question: '*How* should we suffer?' we shall find our answer in this most profound of all mysteries: that it is God who suffers.

To someone who has been torn apart by grief, this comes as an unimaginable consolation. For what it tells us is that we grieve in company with God. I don't mean simply that he walks with us (as it were) but that he himself knows the reality of a grieving Father's heart. He has grieved the death of his Son. And if, as Moltmann suggests, 'the greater the love, the deeper the grief', God must know the greatest depths of all.[14] For what else was the relationship between Father and Son if not pure love? This surely gets him off the hook, though ironically only by remaining on the cross.

But is that where he has to stay? Do we have only a suffering God who helps by virtue of his identification with our pain but who can do nothing about it? This is where I have been helped by the Old Testament scholar Walter Brueggemann. Soon after arriving in Pasadena last April at the start of those awful six weeks following Renee's death, I found myself reading his book *The Bible Makes Sense*. Needless to say, nothing at all made much sense to me back then but I was struck nonetheless by his comment that: 'The way to Easter is Good Friday. The victory of resurrection requires the vulnerability of crucifixion.'[15]

What this means is that the only way to resurrection is through death. Death is the last enemy but its power is broken because, far from being the ogre that can never be beaten, it has already been overthrown by the cross and resurrection of Christ.

[14] Jürgen Moltmann, *The Coming of God* (London: SCM, 1996).

[15] Walter Brueggemann, *The Bible Makes Sense* (Winona MN: St Mary's Press, 1997 edn), p. 98.

Jesus is not only the representative human being in his death but is at the same time the representative human being in his rising. His resurrection is the prototype of humanity's own. Death may for a time apparently win but in fact it is vanquished. Renee is already the conqueror.

Consequently, death is relativised: it becomes the necessary gateway to resurrection life in all its fullness. There simply can be no resurrection without death first. It is the only way. The pattern is clear: no victory without vulnerability; no resurrection without death.

This, of course, is something Renee knew full well. She and I had talked about it several times following her 1998 cancer. It was never the fact of death she feared, only the manner of dying (as, I suspect, do we all). In the event, her ending was merciful and swift – as she wanted.

But at what cost! Her own death may have been pain-free but the consequent pain for the rest of us has seemed at times unbearable. Yet even here the vulnerability-victory/death-resurrection pattern presents itself. For it suggests that we who grieve will one day find new life arising out of death. Our vulnerability will ultimately give way to victory, whatever form that might take.

I realise all this may sound terribly pious and precious; and, believe me Alex, I hate that kind of talk as much as you do. It can sound so disconnected from reality. This is where I have found a second passage from Brueggemann pertinent: 'Jesus and his people always live between the banishment of [Good] Friday and the gathering of [Easter] Sunday, always between the exile of crucifixion and the new community of resurrection.'[16]

This struck me so much that here's what I wrote by way of reflection at the time:

1. Christians have always to confront the reality of death and dying in the world as it is, not in the world as we would like

16 Ibid., p. 94.

it to be. We are, until the Last Day, in-betweeners – people who inhabit an in-between land. We have neither completely escaped the pull of Good Friday nor reached the glory of Easter Day.

2. We nevertheless live in faith – not the fragile wishful thinking that is often associated with that word but the trustful looking-forward that the writer to the Hebrews speaks of: '... the assurance of things hoped for, the conviction of things not seen' (Heb. 11:1). This can only come from God and be sustained by him.

3. Whatever my own future holds, I shall find myself living in the light both of Renee's death and of her resurrection. This will mean that in the state of in-betweenness, grief will always co-exist with hope. The period between Friday and Sunday is lived as tension between each. I shouldn't run away from this but should recognise it for what it is: both gift and task.

None of this is easy but as you see, I haven't departed the Faith and don't intend to. It's theology that is enabling me to make sense of tragedy in the end. There's no neat solution – a kind of theological QED. But how could there be? We're dealing with a double mystery: the existence of suffering in God's good creation; and the truth of divine suffering as a fact of the universe. We may not be content that there seems to be no final answer to fit our canons of intellectual tidiness but I'm relieved that it should be so. I'd rather have mystery than puzzle anyday.

How about you? Which would you prefer? My money's on your being a puzzler. But I could be wrong ...

Francis

Letter 6

Dear Alex,

It's a Tuesday morning in February – wet, windy and dull: typical Bristol weather. As if to match the day outside, I'm sitting here at my desk writing this latest letter, tears streaming down my face, box of Kleenex by my side, observing that I've been ambushed yet again.

It should come as no surprise: last Saturday was Renee's birthday. On Friday – around 12 noon in fact – it will be exactly one year since we received the diagnosis that Renee had cancer of the lung and the liver. In less than a month, it will be the anniversary of her death: more milestones. One by one they pass by …

The theme of love has been much on my mind of late. Inevitably so, I think, given that the memories of her final weeks are now surfacing. From time to time, people ask me whether we were able to say goodbye. I always answer yes but point out that we never used the word. The occasion was a Wednesday evening – February the 19th to be exact. It was the last full day she spent at home; within twenty-four hours she would be in hospital for the final time; in twelve days she would be dead.

Wednesday had not been good. Renee simply couldn't stay awake for more than a few seconds. No sooner did she begin a conversation than it trailed off as she fell asleep. The doctor was unsure why this was so. Maybe it was the medication, maybe the cancer.

On Wednesday evenings Trinity College celebrates its weekly communion service. Earlier in the day, the tutor responsible had phoned to ask whether we would like communion brought to the house afterwards. At first, I hesitated, thinking that Renee might not be up to it. But in the end I agreed. After all, Reg (a family friend staying with us at the time) and I would appreciate it.

Looking back, I can see this was one of those conversations that was arranged by God. Two women students – Jackie and Hilary – arrived at about 8.00 pm (I think). Together, the five of us shared bread and wine around Renee's bedside as she summoned up the energy to stay awake. My fears that she might not realise what was going on proved to be unfounded as the autopilot inside her kicked in and, professional clergywoman to the end, she firmly said the prayers and responses. It was the last time she was to 'remember the Lord's death' until she came to see him face to face less than two weeks later.

After Jackie and Hilary had left, I sat quietly reading by her bedside as Renee lapsed into sleep again. She hadn't eaten properly for a week since developing thrush in the mouth and so was very weak and dehydrated. After a few minutes, however, she suddenly sat up and I could see that underneath all the layers of tiredness and depletion, her spirit was struggling to communicate something important. Drawing on all her reserves of energy, Renee looked hard at me, fixed me in the eye and then said simply: 'I love you.' I replied, 'I love you too', and she fell asleep once more, her mission completed. We both knew what had just passed. It was our goodbye.

When I think about this incident, I realise it was one of those moments of divine mercy that God graciously gives us from time to time. After she was admitted to hospital the next day, there was never an opportunity to make our farewells. In the public space of the ward, the intimacy would have been difficult, if not impossible. And then she shortly declined into delirium and unconsciousness.

Speaking with one of her close friends later, I also came to realise that despite her debilitation, Renee knew what she was doing. While at home for the last time, she had told her friend that once she went into hospital again, she would never return home; and that she and I were now more in love than ever. She was not afraid of death but she simply didn't want us to part. So on that last Wednesday evening, fully aware that she was dying, she determined to make a final declaration of love while she could. Even now I find this overwhelming.

Twelve days later, at around 8.30 am, Renee went to be with her Lord. It was the feast of the Transfiguration. (I emailed friends with the words: 'As always, her timing was impeccable.') She had been unconscious for six days. Yet in that period, I believe even then she acted out of love in ways that begin to make sense only with hindsight. It seems no coincidence, for example, that she died only a few hours after the last of family and friends had visited. For various reasons, not all of them had been able to get to Bristol previously. But, one by one, they did so through the week. When her closest friend had managed to visit on the final Saturday (and, in fact, had kept a bedside vigil through the night), it was as if Renee decided that the time was right to give up her spirit and so she did. The fact that it was the Lord's Day, the day of resurrection, and the feast of the Transfiguration was, I believe, no coincidence. She and God had it worked out.

At the time, I was also vaguely aware of something else. But not until a few weeks later – during Holy Week – did it dawn on me. I was driving around Pasadena when suddenly a thought struck me: as an act of love, Renee had chosen to give me a precious departing gift. As she gave herself into the hands of God, so she put something into mine.

Let me explain: Renee had for some time blamed herself for the effects of her disability on our lives. Only a few weeks previously, she was distressed that her incapacity and low energy levels prevented us from doing all the things that fully-abled people do. No matter how much I tried to reassure her, she still felt guilty.

Then two days before Good Friday (again, no coincidence I think), I recalled the strong sense I had felt of Renee's reaching out to me at a deep intuitive level as she was dying. It struck me that this had been her way of giving me one last gift: the gift of years – certainly the years past but also the years to come. It was as if she was saying in that straightforward, commonsense way of hers:

> I cannot do anything about my dying. I shall soon be with Christ. But please know that I love you and give you the gift of the future, whatever it might hold. I can't affect it and I won't be part of it; but I bequeath it to you. It is yours to accept and use as God leads. Even in the midst of your sorrow, receive it with my love.

But what does one make of such a gift? It is freedom bought at a terrible price. And at fairly regular intervals I have said to God: 'Thank you very much but it's not worth the cost. I'd rather have Renee back.' How could this tragic event ever be viewed as gift?

Eleven months later, my reflection is that it was not her death that should be seen as gift but the manner of her dying. The grace of God which had characterised her life infused her death. She bore witness to divine love even as she bade farewell to human love. For that I can give thanks.

But I must tell you about one more thing: a final act of love on Renee's part that I discovered four months after she had died. In June, I was preparing material for my summer class at Fuller Theological Seminary when an email arrived inviting me to speak at the seminary's weekly chapel service during my stay. Specifically, would I share something of my grief experience?

After reflection, I agreed and set about choosing a Bible reading. In the end, I decided on a passage from the Song of Songs, chapter 8 verses 5–7, which reminded me so much of Renee, especially in its poignant depiction of a woman leaning on the arm of her lover, just as she did when walking with me.

However, having made my decision, I thought I should check the translation. So I first went to the Jerusalem Bible I had given Renee as a present for her ordination at Southwell Minster in 1994. This seemed an appropriate place to start:

Who is this coming up from the desert
leaning on her lover?

I awakened you under the apple tree,
where your mother conceived you,
where she who bore you conceived you.

Set me like a seal on your heart
like a seal on your arm.
For love is strong as Death,
Passion as relentless as Sheol.
The flash of it is a flash of fire,
a flame of Yahweh himself.
Love no flood can quench,
no torrents drown.
Were a man to offer all his family wealth
to buy love,
contempt is all that he would gain.

Can you imagine my reaction, then, upon discovering that the selfsame verses I had chosen, Renee had already highlighted in pink! What's more, apart from a couple of verses from the book of Micah, these were the only ones marked out in the entire Bible. It was as if she had known I would one day come across them.

What should I make of this? Not coincidence, surely? And when had she done it? I'm pretty sure it wasn't in her last illness. At no time did she seem fit enough. My best guess then and now is that she highlighted this passage sometime after her first brush with cancer in 1998. And that she did it so that when I discovered it I would know the depth of her love – a love more strong than death itself.

So you see why my musings nearly a year on from her death have led me to ponder the theme of love. I can't get away from it: nor do I want to. When I reflect on the events of the last twelve months, what staggers me is how much she loved me, and how undeserved such love was.

These are deep things that are hard to put into words. I don't want to get maudlin or sentimental. After all, it doesn't befit us Englishmen. But I must return to the theme of love-in-grief when I have had more time to think theologically about it. It's too important to leave alone.

Till then,
>Francis

Letter 7

Dear Alex,

'What is love?' you wonder. Ironically, the last person I remember asking this question was Prince Charles when asked if he loved Diana. But – setting that aside – you have, as always, an unerring eye for the questions that really matter. This one must surely rank alongside Pilate's 'What is truth?' and the Philippian jailer's 'What must I do to be saved?' We are back to where I ended my last letter.

I think your question operates on split levels. Much of what I have written over these last weeks has clearly expressed the emotional level. But, as you point out, that's not enough. However much love may be an emotion, it must be viewed as more than that. This brings us to the other level: the analytical.

What's more, I think we have to distinguish two further aspects: love as a human phenomenon and love considered theologically. There are, of course, even more ways of looking at it, such as the ethical or the historical, but let's stick with these two for the time being.

From a phenomenological point of view, I can't say how important it is that we keep on saying as strongly as possible that love is a universal human experience that cannot be reduced to anything else, whether biological instincts, neurological impulses or chemical interaction (although I note the notion of 'chemistry' is often used in connection with falling in love).

In saying this, we fly in the face of postmodern thinking which frowns upon the idea that humans might possess inbuilt universal characteristics or traits simply by virtue of being human. Such thinking prefers instead to see us as culturally constructed, each culture bestowing upon its members its own characteristics. Where these coincide across cultures, so be it. But this is accidental: it is not a matter of being hewn from a common rock, as it were.

We have to resist the spirit of the age on this point and insist that we share a common humanity given by God. This is not to deny that complex cultural and historical forces mould humanity into different shapes; but universally shared characteristics remain. We are not simply artificial constructions, each fashioned by the contingencies of our particular culture and society, mere bundles of cultural ingredients.

Why does this matter? Because when we talk about loving another person, we need to be clear that we are speaking of an act that, whatever its particular expression, is a mark of what it means to be made and loved by God. The alternative is that we are nothing but an assemblage (I use the word advisedly) of biologically determined instincts and desires on one hand and socially conditioned actions and attitudes on the other. And if this is the case, love is no different in principle from other human drives. Stuffing your face with fish and chips or sublimely making love – take your pick. Both are nothing more than instincts. We must avoid this kind of reductionism like the plague.

Do you remember your lectures on Martin Buber? I can't remember whether you took the course with me or with another lecturer. It doesn't matter. The point is that Buber distinguished between two ways of relating. When we relate to inanimate objects (say trees or rocks), the relationship is one of I-It: I relate to these as things, not as persons. They lack the basic features of humanity which in turn derive from the image of God.

When we relate to human beings, however, we relate as I-Thou. For the Other is not a mere It but a person. He/she can be addressed as Thou. When we look at them, we see a reflection of ourselves (hardly possible with a tree or a rock). And what's more important, the Thou regards us likewise so that they, too, see a reflection of themselves. It is a meeting of persons, not things.

When we speak of love, then, we are speaking of a relationship between two beings of the same kind, each capable of mutuality and intimacy in ways that can be experienced only between two Thous. When you ask 'What is love?' this is the answer (or at least part of it).

Why is this way of looking at things important? Let me see if I can illustrate: think back to that couple you told me about last year. What were their names – Kylie and Jason, I believe? Or am I getting mixed up? Anyway, whatever they were called, they came to you for counselling. Their relationship had run out of steam and they wanted to know how to get it back on track.

If I recall rightly, after meeting with them a few times, you suggested that the problem was not lack of novelty (as they thought) but something much deeper: that they had never learned to treat each other as persons rather than as objects. They had begun their relationship with a simple aim: to get as much pleasure out of it as possible and then to move onto someone else when the pleasure ran out (i.e. when they got bored). In short, they were determined to avoid commitment of heart and soul so as to maximise the pleasure and then feel free to run when there was none left.

The problem was that they fell in love. They came to regard each other as more than pleasure machines or sources of gratification. Instead, they actually began to enjoy the other's company for its own sake. They came to delight in each other as persons rather than objects. But because this was such a foreign experience for both of them and one which made a great many more emotional demands, they quickly got into difficulties once the relationship became more than a matter of sensual desire. In short, love came to succeed lust.

Now I don't know if you consciously drew upon Buber as you arrived at this conclusion. But your analysis was pure I-It versus I-Thou. And when you presented it to them, it worked: they understood immediately the choice that faced them and decided to shape their lifestyles so as to reflect the movement from a thing-centred mentality to a person-shaped one. Love conquered in the end.

So much for the phenomenology. I could say a great deal more but I'm pretty sure you're itching to get to the theology. Here goes.

Of all the world religions, it is Christianity that is distinguished by love, beginning with St John's majestic declaration: 'God so loved the world…' (John 3:16). We might add what John omitted: 'even though He didn't need to'. And so we're pointed to love as much more than a purely human phenomenon. It can't be viewed as just another human instinct; for its origin lies in the character and creative-redemptive will of God. We love because he loves. Or, more accurately, we love because he *loved*.

As creatures, then, we are destined for love. We are made in his image, an image which bears the hallmark of love. When asked what God is like, we can do no better than quote St John again: 'God is love.' To love is to do what God does: it's his job.

'Now this is all very fine,' I can hear you say. 'But what does it actually mean to assert that we are destined for love or made in love's image?' Well, for one thing it means that we cannot refuse love. Unless we're emotionally distorted or out of touch with what it is to be human, we shall always seek to give and receive love in some shape or form. Indeed, when we speak of somebody as a psychopath or a sociopath, we invariably refer to their inability to give or receive love. They are simply incapable of doing either. To love is the essence of being created in God's image.

But there's a lot more to it than this. To say that love flows from our being his image-bearers is accurate but a bit abstract. Let's try a different tack. When we look at Scripture, there's surely one thing about God that hits us between the eyes: that he loves intensely, passionately and wholly. He's portrayed as Israel's lover, her husband, who when betrayed desperately wants her back and is prepared to be ever-forgiving as he stands with open arms. His love for her is unlimited, even when she casts him aside to play the harlot. Even in judgement, love persists.

To say that we bear his image, then, is to say that we are capable of the same kind of love. At this point, theologians and philosophers usually point out that there are many different kinds of love (signified by a variety of biblical words) and that it's crucial we understand which kind we're talking about. Now this may be true – confusing brotherly love with erotic love, for example, could prove a serious category error – but I want to argue that in all types of love there must be one characteristic that runs throughout. I mean, of course, the readiness to be self-giving for the sake of the other, to see them as valuable in themselves, to desire their best, to be willing to go the second mile not because it may profit *us* but because it will profit *them*. This is gift-love and the cross is the paradigm.

As you know, the term *agape* sums this up. But I hope you can see that these qualities are fundamental to all the other kinds of love as well if they are to be judged true love, whether between brother and sister, mother and son, daughter and father, friend and friend, or lover and lover. Wanting the best for the other person and being ready to seek it is the hallmark of a love that reflects the divine.

Now much theological ink has been spilt over the clash between *agape* and another Greek term for love, namely *eros*. *Agape*, it's contended, is the better of the two because it is interested in the other person in themselves, not for what they can give in return. It has no motive outside itself. It doesn't act because it finds something worth having in the other but simply because it cares for them. It seeks no reward. The one who is the object of *agape* may be the most horrible person in the world: *agape* still seeks their best.

Eros, by contrast, is reckoned to be an acquisitive love. It strives for what it hasn't got and is restless till it gets it. It's egocentric, offering love only to those whom it values for what they can provide, for their ability to satisfy. Hence the modern equation of the erotic with sexual satisfaction.

The church, influenced by Plato, has traditionally accepted

this distinction. And there's something in it. But I think I want to caution against accepting it too readily or uncritically. As we've seen, it's no accident (if we believe in Scripture as divine revelation) that the imagery of human erotic love is used to describe the relationship between God and his people. Put more provocatively, does our picture of divine love allow us to imagine God as the lover? The one who longs to make love passionately and tenderly to his wife – not as a fulfilment of desire but as a sign of intimate self-giving?

What I'm arguing for is an understanding of love as something that shares characteristics of both *agape* and *eros*. In fact, this is exactly what happens when two people fall in love. There's nothing they won't do for each other. No task is too much, no request too great. Indeed, these are seen not as demands but as opportunities. The most trivial and humdrum chores are transformed into moments of transcendent delight. Each wants to give him or herself to the other, not out of self interest but just because they are there. Their mutual pleasure is simply in being with each other for its own sake. In some mysterious way, lovers desire their beloved not for the thrill they can give but simply for themselves.

As usual, C. S. Lewis puts it well: writing against those who see 'falling in love' merely as a function of the sexual drive, he observes that,

> Very often what comes first is simply a delighted preoccupation with the Beloved – general, unspecified preoccupation with her in her totality. A man in this state really hasn't leisure to think of sex. He is too busy thinking of a person. The fact that she is a woman is far less important than the fact that she is herself ... If you asked him what he wanted, the true reply would often be, 'To go on thinking of her.' He is love's contemplative.[17]

17 C. S. Lewis, *The Four Loves* (London: Geoffrey Bles, 1960), p. 108.

But note how easily this can be blended with *agape*. The kind of love Lewis describes as *eros* carries within it the qualities of *agape* too: self-giving, desirous of the best for the other, valuing them intrinsically. The neat distinction between *agape* and *eros* turns out to be not so neat after all.

Of course, falling in love is only the first stage. If love is to mature into sustainable mutual self-giving it must deepen and grow. But this only means that *eros* must listen carefully to *agape* and allow itself to be moulded and shaped by it.

For me, the marvel is that in her last days, Renee demonstrated how much love truly is a blend of the two. Her self-giving, her delight in our being with each other, her final gift of the future – all these remind me how she bore the divine image of love, all other loves excelling. I find myself lost in wonder, love and praise both for her and for our God of grace.

Francis

Letter 8

Dear Alex,

So you found my reflections on love helpful? Good. But now you're wondering how I am? How these extended musings on love leave me feeling? I came across a poem recently that I remember reading shortly after Renee's funeral. It's by Norah Leney:

> Deep sobs –
> That start beneath my heart
> And hold my body in a grip that hurts.
> The lump that swells inside my throat
> Brings pain that tries to choke.
> Then tears course down my cheeks –
> I drop my head in my so empty hands
> Abandoning myself to deep dark grief
> And know that with the passing time
> Will come relief.
> That though the pain may stay
> There will soon come a day
> When I can say her name and be at peace.[18]

The truth is: I fear that day is not so far away. I say 'fear' because the prospect evokes such complex emotions within me that it's tempting to stick with the simplicity of pain. It has, after all, been my companion now for so long. To be able to say Renee's name and be at peace is a prospect that is both liberating and frightening.

[18] Norah Leney, 'Grief', in *All in the End is Harvest*, ed. Agnes Whitaker (London: Darton, Longman & Todd, 2001 edn), p 15.

But there's a deeper reason for my apprehension. I think it can best be summed up like this: if it's the case that 'the greater the love, the greater the grief,' does the diminution of grief mean that I love her less? I cannot bear the thought. It would seem like a betrayal: 'Okay, mate, the year's up. You've done your time – you can move on now. Nothing you can do will bring her back. You've got a life to live. No sense in mourning forever. She wouldn't want you to mope around.'

The trouble is: I can see great sense in these words. It *is* a year; I can't bring her back; I do have to move forward; Renee would want to see an end to the grief. But I still find myself occasionally wondering whether love requires that I stay where I am and that I would be loving her less if I didn't.

In my heart of hearts I know this isn't the case. We do, after all, resist something or somebody hardest just before we are about to change tack. But it doesn't help that the grief literature uses such language as 'emotional disinvestment and reinvestment' to convey the idea that one's emotions aren't static. I find this kind of talk so conceptually abominable that – even setting aside the sheer ugliness of the language – it makes me want to vomit. To reduce the depth and richness of human love to the language of commercial transaction is to behave as if the only discourse that matters is that of economics: that, as Marx and Engels observed, everything ends up being reduced to the cash nexus. How can you possibly think or speak of something which is depictable only by the language of aesthetics as if it were no more than a commodity?

Maybe I'm being too sensitive. After all, as we discussed some weeks ago, it does feel different now. The metaphors I used to describe the intensity of grief in those first months are much less intrusive and powerful. The 'deep sobs' described by Norah Leney are not nearly so frequent or long-lasting. Even standing at the graveside last Saturday, I didn't feel in the depths as I did even a few weeks ago. I can begin to anticipate the 'day when I can say her name and be at peace'. Not perhaps the whole day yet but at least its dawning. Or maybe the pre-dawn when the pitch darkness of the night is no longer so deep but the sky hasn't yet lightened.

Does this mean my love for Renee has diminished? The more I think about it, the less I think it does. Those who know about these things – the psychologists and counsellors – are of one mind: that there comes a time in the grieving process when the collapse of the old world begins to give way to the construction of the new. And part of this is the transformation of the griever's love for the deceased. No longer is it merely a painful memory: it becomes an integral part of the new self that is emerging from the emotional wreckage. Here's another poem:

> I had thought that your death
> Was a waste and a destruction,
> A pain of grief hardly to be endured.
> I am only beginning to learn
> That your life was a gift and a growing
> And a loving left with me.
> The desperation of death
> Destroyed the existence of love,
> But the fact of death
> Cannot destroy what has been given.
> I am learning to look at your life again
> Instead of your death and your departing.[19]

What does this transformation involve? To be sure, it is born only in pain; or, to change the image, there is no short cut through the long valley of the shadow. But the important thing is that love remains: nothing can undermine or remove it. It is a 'love stronger than death'. So I do continue to love Renee but with a different kind of love. Not an idealised love which

[19] Marjorie Pizer, 'The Existence of Love', in *All in the End is Harvest*, p. 118.

ring-fences her memory in some sort of immutable and unreachable shrine; but a love which recognises that she has gone and which consequently honours and treasures her for who she was and who she continues to be in the life of God. St John Chrysostom summed it up best, I think, when he said that 'He whom we love and lose is no longer where he was before. He is now wherever we are.'[20]

So where (and how) does that leave me? A couple of letters back, I wrote in tears; but now I find myself with a sense of wonder that in such a short space of time I should have moved in my mood and self-expression from darkness to at least the glimmerings of light. I can begin to see that love never ends, even though it may change and evolve.

Or to use a metaphor offered to me by Edward Bailey, the priest who conducted Renee's funeral, the sadness that covered the ground like a never-lifting dew at the beginning of grief has given way to gathered clouds which shed their moisture from time to time but do not dominate everything. Sometimes they shed a great deal but increasingly the downpour is less intense and of shorter duration. When it pours, it soaks me but the intervals between showers is growing longer. What's more, there appears blue sky and even sunshine much more often. This is not the end. It is not even the beginning of the end. But it is perhaps the end of the beginning. Renee's gift of years is already at work.

Your brother in Christ,
Francis

[20] Quoted in Elizabeth Collick, *Through Grief: The Bereavement Journey* (London: Darton, longman & Todd, 1986), p. 85.

Looking Back

How does one conclude a book such as this? Its story and subject matter have been so highly personal that it is tempting simply to sign off and leave readers to draw their own conclusions, especially where my narrative has in some way touched theirs. But I am a reflective person by nature and find it hard not to offer some final thoughts about what has without doubt been the worst time of my life. I do so in the hope that, as with the rest of the book, they may have something to say to those who struggle with similar questions and issues.

But how to organise such reflections? At the end of 1 Corinthians 13, St Paul reminds his readers that 'there are three things that last for ever: faith, hope and love. But the greatest of these is love' (verse 13, NEB). In what follows I shall structure my thoughts around this famous Pauline trilogy.

Faith

There have been times during the last fifteen months when faith has been hard and doubt has threatened to overwhelm. This doubt has not taken a simple form – I have never been tempted to reject the *existence* of God, for example. At no time did I ever find myself wondering whether God was just a figment of the imagination: I faced that question some years ago when Renee first became disabled; and I concluded then that to imagine a universe without God offered no hope – only meaninglessness and despair. Rather, the doubt has been more nuanced and subtle than that: my repeated question has been: '*What kind of* God should I continue to believe in?' In the light of the dreadful experience I had undergone, how credible was the image of God I had inherited and built up over the years? Was it anything more than a convenient prop? It was this kind of doubt that lay behind the diatribe expressed in Letter 3.

Paradoxically, it is often when we feel our faith to be at its weakest that it is, in fact, at its most strong. For if there is one thing that has grown throughout this period, it has been my theology of gracious gift. I shall return to this later in my discussion of love; but for now, let me explain a little more.

From the moment of Renee's diagnosis, I experienced two strong feelings: firstly, that she would not recover (though I had no sense of how far ahead her death lay); and secondly, that God would somehow meet me in the midst of the pain I was beginning to experience and which I knew was to come. Exactly how he would do this, I didn't know: I simply intuited it. In the event, both feelings turned out to be true.

These two intuitions led me not only into an intellectual but an emotional paradox. At one and the same time, I was conscious both of the tragedy that lay ahead and of the ways in which God's gift of grace to face the struggle was being offered and strengthened. I found myself holding two very powerful sets of feelings in tension: sadness, sorrow and impending bleakness on one hand; and awareness of God's presence on the other. It was the combination of these that was to dominate my emotional journey for the next twelve months.

So faith, for me, during this period came to mean not so much the intellectual content of belief (*The* Faith), as a mode of somewhat precarious being. That God existed, I had no doubt. That the picture of God portrayed by the Christian Faith was intellectually credible and coherent, I continued to accept. But as to the *emotional* credibility of such a God – that was where the existential issue lay. This was to be the centre of the spiritual working through of my grief over the next year.

Hope

Hope is one of those words that can mean something or nothing. In contemporary culture, it is often associated with a kind of wishful thinking underlain by doubt: 'Oh, I do hope that Jim's job is secure,' cries the wife whose husband's post is threatened by reorganisation within his firm. 'We cannot be sure but we hope this round of chemotherapy will reverse the cancer's growth,' explains the oncologist to her patient.

But, from a biblical perspective, hope is not a matter of human aspiration but of God's faithfulness to his promises. To Abraham, the example *par excellence* in both Old and New Testaments, God promised a series of seemingly impossible things: a land (Gen. 12:7; 13:15; 15:7, 18); descendants (15:18–19); and unlimited blessing (17:4–6). At times, Abraham proved extremely full of doubt. Had it been left to him (as the example of Hagar showed), Abraham would have been tempted to fulfil God's promises in his own way.

Despite the temptation, however, Abraham proved faithful. Caught in the tension between the 'now' of unfulfilled promise and the 'not yet' of God bringing his word to pass, Abraham in the end trusted God and was counted righteous for doing so. In St Paul's words, he 'gave honour to God, in the firm conviction of his power to do what he had promised' (Rom 4:21, NEB).

It is significant that Abraham received God's promises of hope by means of God's direct word to him. On two occasions I was conscious of the same thing happening to me. The first took place in Suffolk in the early summer of 2003. I had returned from my six weeks in the USA following Renee's funeral and was driving towards Bury St Edmunds to visit my aunt when, without much thought, I inserted a CD into the player. I had no idea what it contained other than a collection of classical pieces. The disc had belonged to Renee.

After a few minutes, up came Kathleen Ferrier's rendering of Psalm 37. As she sang the words, tears streamed down my face for it seemed as if God were speaking directly into my sadness and sorrow: 'Trust in the Lord and do good ... Commit your way to the Lord; trust in him and he will act ... Rest in the Lord and wait patiently for him.' So powerful was the emotion these words engendered that I had to pull over and wait a while before continuing on.

The second experience occurred in June while visiting Robert and Meg Forrest, two good friends who live near Inverness in Scotland. Robert had been a Faculty member at Trinity till the previous year and Meg had been Renee's closest friend in Bristol. The visit was a reflective and sombre one, full of tears and talk. One day, while walking by the local river, I sat down alongside the water and quietly prayed. I was feeling particularly sad that day. Not only was the inner emptiness still overwhelming but I couldn't envisage a future that would feel any different. Remembering my earlier discussions with G in Pasadena to the effect that the grief journey would last at least a year, I felt like a prisoner locked in his cell serving his time as he waited to be freed.

It was at this point that God gave me an alternative way of looking at things. I clearly remember that (in the midst of praying) an instant switch took place. No longer (it became clear) should I regard the period that lay ahead as one of imprisonment: instead it was to be a time of preparation. I had no idea for what – simply that God was going to use the months ahead for a purpose he had yet to disclose. The effect of this realisation was the same as it had been when I heard Kathleen Ferrier. Not prison but preparation. I found myself weeping.

Looking back, I remain as I did then: grateful for God's mercies in which he gives us experiences of himself and his loving care in unmistakable ways. Like Abraham, I was being invited to trust God for the future, whatever it might hold.

These two events reminded me that Christian hope is rooted in a twofold reality: the reality of God's promises; and the reality of personal encounter with him. In the many bouts of intense grief I was to experience over the coming months, I found myself recalled to these moments of God's presence and promise: hope for the future rooted in God's acts of the past. In Moltmann's words, the essential truth about God 'lies in the statement "Faithful is he that promised."'

Love

If faith and hope have been two fundamental aspects of my grief journey so has the reality of love. It can be expressed in the following paradox: in the midst of the most profound sense of loss, I have rediscovered my theology of gracious gift in ways that I would not have thought possible. To use Julian's terminology, the 'revelation of divine love' has been a constant feature throughout. It is this that has enabled me to struggle out of Gethsemane, time after time and it is this that has been the greatest gift of all.

But how has such love been revealed? At times, it has been through direct encounter with God, as my Suffolk and Scottish experiences showed. But mostly it has been through *human* love shown in numerous acts of compassion large and small. In these, God's love has been made real. It has been incarnated in human actions. This has enabled me to reflect again on the evangelical tradition from which I come (and gladly continue to own). Here, it is frequently assumed that we experience the love of God most powerfully when (to use John Wesley's vivid phrase) our hearts are 'strangely warmed'. Yet, for me, despite the occurrence of some experiences of this sort, the strongest and most overpowering examples of God's love have been when others have shown me human love and kindness. In their humanity they have revealed the human face of God. More often than not, these have taken place when my heart has been anything but warmed.

I shouldn't be surprised by this. The principle of incarnate love – revealed supremely in Jesus Christ – means that it is precisely when we are at our lowest ebb, when the absence of God seems greatest, when our hearts feel empty, that divine love is actively seeking us out. Jesus, as the incarnate Son of God, did exactly this in his earthly ministry; and by his Spirit, he continues to do the same now. Christianity is built around the truth of the incarnation.

And so it has proved in my own experience. The gift of God

I have treasured most since Renee's death has been the gift of *people* who have been willing to demonstrate their love. It has been in them rather than in quasi-mystical experiences that I have experienced the love of God at work. And I remain thankful to God for sending so many of them my way.

Interestingly, he has done so by means of *communities* of faith. Although God's love has been shown in the actions of in-dividuals, it is significant that they have been members of communities with which I already had some kind of identity and of which I already felt a part: Trinity College Bristol, St Michael's, Winterbourne, St Mark's, Woodthorpe (where I served as vicar from 1990–99), Fuller Theological Seminary, St Mark's, Altadena. From the moment Renee was diagnosed, friends and colleagues from all of these stepped in to help and in doing so demonstrated the love of God incarnate. It is as if God was saying, 'I will not leave you alone. I am with you by my Spirit whom I have given to each of these communities and to each of these people. I will walk with you through their companionship.'

As I have reflected on this, I have come to realise afresh that the principle of incarnation means that we must look for God in the ordinary as well as the extraordinary things of life. His love is at work in those 'countless acts of love' of which the hymn writer speaks as daily experiences. Although God may be present in the spiritual 'whiz-bangs', he is also active in the little things too. He is in the small still voice as well as the rushing wind.

And so I am immensely grateful for those friends from Nottingham and Bristol who took me in hand in the twenty-three days leading to Renee's death and in the week or so up to her funeral; for my American brothers and sisters who took me into their hearts and homes (even though they scarcely knew me) during the six weeks in April and May when the intensity of grief was at its greatest and when I was at my most vul-nerable; for my Australian friends who happened to visit Bristol on my birthday – the first since Renee died – and who so sensitively helped me through it; for the students of Fuller Theological Seminary last summer who demonstrated their capacity for pastoral care by caring for their visiting British lecturer; and, perhaps most of all, for the members of Trinity College who have prayed for and supported me daily through the long, dark months of loss and grief. In the loving acts of them all, I have known the love of God at its most profound. They are the reason I can say that my theology of divine gift has been strengthened. Without them I would not be writing this book.

Conclusion

I began this chapter by speaking of faith, hope and love. It may seem strange to speak of these alongside a picture of grief as anger, hopelessness and despair. How can I reconcile the two? Therein lies the paradox. In the midst of human emotions of the most overwhelming kind, it is possible to know God. For he is to be found not by avoiding or sanitising our humanity but by embracing it. He enfolds our emotions, however negative, in his love and deals gently with them. He does not leave us or forsake us, whatever our feelings might tell us. And he does not desert us because we express them honestly. As I have discovered, it is in the storm centre of confusion and pain that he meets us. He dwells *in* the cloud of unknowing, not around the other side of it. He invites us to discover him there, even though to do so may be terrifying. It is an awesome and challenging thought.